C000061777

CREATED TO BE WHOLE

Other books in this series by the same authors:

Created for Love –
Understanding and building self-esteem
(Eagle, 1994).

Created for Intimacy –
Discovering intimacy with yourself, others and God
(Eagle, 1996).

CREATED TO BE WHOLE

John and Agnes Sturt

eagle

Guildford, Surrey

Copyright © 1998 John and Agnes Sturt

The rights of John and Agnes Sturt to be identified as authors of this work has been asserted by them in accordance with the Copyright, Design and Patents Act 1988.

British Library Cataloguing in Publication Data. A catalogue record for this book is available from the British Library.

Published by Eagle, an imprint of Inter Publishing Service (IPS) Ltd, PO Box 530, Guildford, Surrey GU2 5FH.

Scripture quotations noted NIV are taken from the HOLY BIBLE, NEW INTERNATIONAL VERSION. Copyright © 1973, 1978, 1984 by the International Bible Society. Used by permission of Hodder & Stoughton, a Division of Hodder Headline.

Typeset by Eagle Publishing
Printed by Cox & Wyman, Reading

ISBN No: 0 86347 276 1

CONTENTS

Acknowledgements   7
Introduction   9

PART I UNDERSTANDING WHOLENESS
Summary

One   'Wholth'   13
Two   'Illth'   39
Three   Blocks and Keys to Wholeness   66

PART II DEVELOPING WHOLENESS
Summary

Four   Physical Wholeness   87
Five   Intellectual Wholeness   112
Six   Emotional Wholeness   137
Seven   Social Wholeness   162
Eight   Spiritual Wholeness   186
Nine   Towards Wholeness and Maturity   210

Appendix: Relaxation Exercises   221
Notes and References   225
Subject Index
Selected Bibliography   239
Scripture References   2444

Dedicated to Christy,
a brave little boy who lived his short life to the full.

ACKNOWLEDGEMENTS

This book has been years in the making, as we discovered, explored, taught and tried to apply these principles of living to our own lives. Our teachers have been many, and we acknowledge them frequently throughout the text, not only to express our gratitude, but also to provide a resource for others to draw on.

Specifically, we express our appreciation to those who carefully critiqued the manuscript: Joyce Huggett, Rev John McAlpine, Helen Stevenson, Rev Roger Elley-Brown, Steve and Elaine McFadzean, Cilla Potter and Sue Wavre. We value the help and advice of others: Sheila Pritchard, Geoff and Gail Stevens, Dr George Trew, Dr John Hitchen, Dr Peter Lineham and Harry Downes MD.

There are no writers, only 're-writers', and we are grateful to those who have helped us in this task. We also want to thank David Wavre, our publisher, for his encouragement in bringing this book to birth, and Pat Bish for the cover design and art work.

INTRODUCTION

As we come to the end of our seventh decade in life, the topic of this book has become increasingly important to us. Becoming a whole person and helping others on this journey has been our goal for many years. Judging by the many books that have been written, and the thousands of web sites on Internet relating to wholeness and wellness, there is much interest worldwide in these topics.

Someone has said: 'Who we *are* is God's gift to us; who we *become* is our gift to God.' Whole people keep growing to maturity in all aspects of their lives. All parts of our person need attention in order to become whole in a balanced way.

In **Part I** we define wholeness, wellness and shalom. We call this 'wholth', and contrast it with the opposite state, 'illth'. In **Part II** we focus in turn on the five major areas of our person. It is somewhat artificial to divide ourselves into five parts, because they all overlap. However, it is helpful to address each area specifically.

We invite you to join us on this quest for wholeness. Wholeness does not suddenly happen to us but is a process. This book reflects some of our own journey, and includes material that we have taught in seminars and workshops over the past twenty years or so. We freely acknowledge how much we have learned from books, and especially from people that we have worked with individually or in small groups.

Created to be Whole is the final part of a trilogy, written as a series of 'workbooks' for personal growth and development. They are designed for people to use on their own, in small groups or to work through with the help of a counsellor. *Created for Love* addresses the fundamental issue of how we feel about ourselves, and how we can develop a healthy sense of self-worth. *Created for Intimacy* moves on from there to explore ways of making a good relationship with other people and with God. *Created to be Whole* builds on these two, and explores how to become a whole, mature and balanced person: physically, intellectually, emotionally, socially and spiritually.

We would welcome correspondence with you if you wish to contact us.

John and Agnes Sturt

211b, St Andrews Road
Epsom, Auckland
New Zealand

E-mail < johnsturt@compuserve.com>

PART I

UNDERSTANDING WHOLENESS

The first three chapters explore the concept of wholeness, how to achieve it, and what prevents us from becoming whole people.

Chapter One
Wholeness, or 'wholth', is defined and then explored by looking at a number of models. The standard Western medical approach is compared with the Wellness model. We examine some psychological perspectives which contribute to our understanding of wholeness. The Jewish and the Christian models of wholeness are briefly considered.

Chapter Two
This chapter looks at 'illth', the opposite of 'wholth'. Many modern lifestyle factors, as well as personal 'drivers' contribute to loss of wholeness in people's lives. The balance between stress and distress and the factors leading to burnout are explored. A practical way of assessing personal burnout, and ways to prevent this condition are outlined.

Chapter Three
A number of factors which can block our journey to wholeness are explored. We also define keys for growing to wholeness.

ONE

'WHOLTH'

As long as you live, keep learning how to live.
Seneca [1]

Tony felt trapped. He was stuck in a job that gave him little satisfaction, apart from providing sufficient income to pay the bills and mortgage. He was now forty-two, married and with three demanding teenagers. He and Jan were growing apart in their relationship, and had little real communication with one another or their children these days. Family life had become a struggle, not a pleasure. He found himself returning home later and later from work each night, sometimes stopping at the pub on the way. He was unfit and even mowing their small lawn left him breathless, which was not surprising as this was about his only exercise.

The vision of life that he once had was gone, and his world seemed to be folding in on him rather than expanding. Tony had been convinced that life had some meaning and purpose, but now was not sure – maybe he had lost his way. He was afraid to share his feelings of failure and despair with his few friends. Jan regarded his reflections as neurotic. There seemed to be no one to turn to. They attended church as a family quite frequently, but did not find it relevant to their daily lives.

Jan was a practical person. If she had thoughts like Tony's, she did not dwell on them but just got on with life. There was a family to feed, a house to maintain, elderly parents to care for and little time for introspection. 'If you don't think about it, perhaps it will go away', was her motto. As the eldest of six children, she had learned early in life to ignore her own needs. Her younger brother had cerebral palsy and she had been expected to take a major part in his care.

Marrying at nineteen removed her from this situation, but put paid to her dream of a career in nursing. It was a hard decision to make, but she had hoped that marriage with Tony would provide the fulfilment she was looking for. They had never discussed together their expectations of marriage, or of one another. Now such conversations were too painful and usually led to a fight.

Many of us can identify with some of the experience of these two people, whether we are stuck in a routine or have a life full of challenge and excitement. The truth is, its not what we do that matters but who we *are*. It is not what we achieve that defines us as human beings but who we are *becoming*. This process of growing and becoming involves change. The only person I can change is myself, and no one can do that work for me. But like Tony and Jan, many people do not know how to go about it. Where do we start? How do we want to be different? It is easy to identify the pain and bleakness of life, but what are the options? We will meet Tony and Jan later and follow their journey towards wholeness.

WHOLENESS

Health and wholeness, which we abbreviate to 'wholth',[2] is the opposite of how Tony and Jan described their worlds. Life for a whole person is expanding rather than contracting. Whole people are not free from problems and difficulties but these become challenges to them rather than threats. Wholeness can be simply defined as:

*To be growing in all areas of life: physically,
intellectually, emotionally, socially and spiritually.*

This does not mean that we have 'arrived' or are perfect, but that we are not stuck in any significant aspect
of life. Whole people are open to growth, development
and change. Their lives are characterised by unity not
disintegration, inter-connectedness rather than isolation. Figure 1.1 identifies the five main aspects of the
whole person. The dotted lines indicate that we cannot
totally compartmentalise these parts of the personality,
and there is considerable overlap between them. The
circles symbolise expansion and growth in all areas.

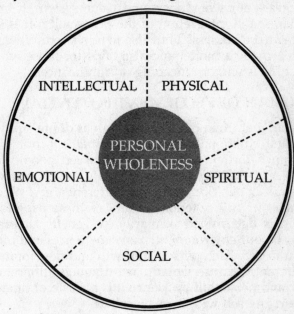

Figure 1.1. A model of wholeness

Life is a journey, not a destination. Psychiatrist and
author, M. Scott Peck, expressed it this way: 'All my life

I used to wonder what I would become. Then about seven years ago I realised that I was never going to grow up – that growing up is an ever on-going process.'[3]

The word *whole* comes from the Old English word *hal*, from which we derive a range of modern English words:

whole, heal, health, holy (hallowed),
holiday, hale (as in hale-and-hearty), Hail!

These words share a common theme relating to health and wellbeing in terms of individuals and relationships. Being whole does not only refer to the body but to the soul. Health and holiness belong together. This includes our world view and value system. It implies balance and integration of the personality. It is something to be possessed but also to be shared. Whole people provide a model and also hope for those who feel that life is without meaning or significance.

HUMAN DEVELOPMENT POTENTIAL

We all mature in the five major areas of life – physical, mental, emotional, social and spiritual. Of course, there is much individual variation between people in the speed of their growth, personality development and the rate of deterioration in the different areas. We never reach our full potential in any of these aspects. The limit is determined primarily by genetic factors, but also by our environment, past experiences and motivation in life. Each person's growth and development is different, because we all have uniquely different gifting and personalities. Hence it is a waste of time comparing myself with someone else.[4]

Healthy people maintain a balance in their development. While we all have greater endowments in some areas than in others, to neglect any of the five major aspects of life leads to imbalance. For example, it is possible to be an intellectual genius but emotionally and socially stunted; to be fully developed and physically fit but spiritually immature. The following is a brief overview of the five dimensions of human growth, which will be more fully developed in subsequent chapters.

Physical Growth
Our physical height and size are pre-determined genetically, but we can be prevented from reaching our potential through illness or malnutrition. Growth starts at conception, not birth. It is affected by the supply of nutrients and oxygen as well as by negative factors such as drugs and infections to which the baby may be exposed prenatally. The initial rapid growth spurt slows down in mid-childhood, then picks up again at puberty. Maximum growth is usually achieved by the early twenties. From then on it is downhill, especially if we neglect the care of our bodies.

Our physical fitness can be nurtured and even increased in adult life through training and healthy nutrition. However, physical deterioration is inevitable with age, and few people in their forties can compete physically with those in their twenties. From about the age of thirty, physiologists estimate that the human body deteriorates at the rate of about one per cent per annum. After about the age of seventy, sometimes earlier, there is a more rapid drop off in physical ability due to degenerative processes or illness.

Intellectual Maturity
The capacity of the human brain is enormous. It contains up to 100 billion neurones, each with hundreds of connections with other cells. Intellectual development is most rapid during the first few years of life, when children have so much to absorb and learn about the world around them. We probably reach our maximum mental capacity in early adult life, although with increasing maturity intellectual ability can grow.

As with the rest of the body, the brain also deteriorates. It has been estimated that an adult loses about 100,000 brain cells a day,[5] but so many cells remain that we are fully capable of normal thinking well into old age. As we move past the sixth decade or so, the brain is increasingly susceptible to damage from decreasing blood supply, as well as such illnesses as Alzheimer's disease. Researchers consider that the average person utilises only about ten per cent of their brain potential in their lifetime.

Emotional Growth

Young children are emotionally free and share their emotions in an uninhibited way, until they learn from adults that to be honest about their emotions is 'bad'. Many parents are frightened by and try to control a child's emotional freedom, and so children often repress their emotions for survival. Of course, children need to learn how to control their emotions appropriately. In teenagers, emotions can be labile and out of control, partly as a result of hormonal changes. Some adults have learned to repress emotions altogether, but healthy people make use of and control their emotions.

In some cultures, especially in the West, emotional expression is regarded as weakness and inappropriate for males particularly. Some people struggle with heavy emotions such as anger, anxiety and depression, and these can dominate and spoil their lives and relationships. However, we can all develop the ability to be comfortable with and use our emotions right through to the end of life.

Social Developement

Our social development is strongly influenced by cultural factors. We are not born with social skills and our ability in this area largely reflects our experiences in the family in which we grew up. However, social skills can be developed at any stage in life, and are closely linked with emotional freedom, intellectual growth and a healthy spirituality. The ability to relate well to others grows out of a mature understanding of oneself. You cannot give away what you do not possess. Social maturity is determined essentially by the degree to which we are able to be 'other-centred' rather than self-centred, and the importance we place on relationships.

Spiritual Growth

The term 'spirituality' is used by different people in a variety of ways. In the past it referred almost entirely to religious matters pertaining to God and to the soul. More recently it has become an inclusive term embracing anything to do with one's philosophy of life, inner being or lifestyle. In a real sense, all things are spiritual, and a division between 'secular' and 'spiritual' is artificial. Tielhard de Chardin expressed it well: 'We are not human beings having a spiritual experience, but spiritual beings having a human experience.'[6] Neglecting our spiritual development starves the essence of who we are. We have personally found that the most profound way to grow spiritually is by experiencing a relationship with God through Christ. This discovery has helped us to know ourselves better, and provided the desire to become the people we were created to be.

While it is helpful to look at each of these five areas separately, we must not lose sight of the fact that we are a whole. Each section of our lives affects all the others, and if one aspect is underdeveloped the whole ecosystem suffers. Mahatma Gandhi observed, 'We cannot do right in one department of life while doing wrong in any other department. Life is a whole.'[7] Gandhi was very impressed by Christian teaching at one stage in his life, but it appears from his writings that he was put off the Christian faith by the inconsistency he saw in the lives of some Christians he met.

19

There are a number of paradigms of wholeness. We will look briefly at five of them: medical, wellness, psychological, Jewish and Christian models.

MEDICAL MODELS

Medical World View Alternatives

The World Health Organisation defines health as 'A state of physical, mental and social well-being, not merely the absence of disease'. This is a statement with which most medical and health workers would agree. But in practice, almost all the focus of Western medicine is placed on dealing with physical health matters, and it is assumed that if a person is free of illness then mental and social health will follow. Certainly it is hard to give any consideration to mental, social or aesthetic aspects of life if I do not have enough food to survive or am suffering from a major illness.

Our eyes were opened to a new understanding of this in 1959, when we went to work in the West Sepik Province of Papua New Guinea. We had been allocated an area of jungle, several days walk from the coast, in which to develop a medical programme. The land included a flat section near a river bed which was large enough for building an airstrip so that we could bring in supplies. The surrounding population had had little contact with the outside world and were just emerging from a stone-age civilisation. My goal was to establish a small, efficient base hospital and a community health programme. Agnes started infant welfare clinics in the villages and shared in the training of medical orderlies.

It took many months to build adequate trust with the local tribes, but gradually they began to bring in sick people. What would irritate me, however, was when very ill patients were carried past the front door of the hospital, over the air strip and across the river to see the other 'doctor' first. Taro was the local medical practitioner or 'witch-doctor', with a powerful reputation. After he had been consulted, patients were carried back to our hospital to see what the white-man's medicine had to offer.

Sometimes the river was in flood, so patients from villages on our side could not cross to visit Taro but were admitted straight to hospital. After a while I realised that we had a controlled experiment in the wards: some patients who had seen the witch-doctor first and others with similar conditions who had not been able to do so. I observed that people who had already attended Taro's clinic recovered more quickly with our treatment than those who had come to us first. What was he providing that was missing from our care?

Eventually, I realised that he and I were seeing our patients from different perspectives. I wanted to know *what* was wrong with them – I had back-up facilities such as a laboratory and x-ray to help make a diagnosis. Taro had not even heard of bacteria and viruses. In fact, he was suffering from leprosy, for which he was obliged to come to me for treatment each week. He wanted to know *why* people were sick. Had they offended some relative (alive or dead) or perhaps a spirit in the jungle? He would perform a magic ritual to try to restore the relationship that had been broken, which dealt with the problem within the framework of their world view.

It was not necessary for me to accept all of his belief system to appreciate the impact of the wider world on the development of an individual's illness. So-called 'primitive' medicine starts with the person and looks at his or her environment and relationships for the cause of illness. This is an *expansionist* process. Western medicine starts with the patient, then focuses on the system or organ that is disordered in a *reductionist* process. If the diagnosis is not obvious from clinical or perhaps x-ray examination, then the biochemistry of the organ is examined through blood tests. In this way, the 'what' is usually discovered but seldom the 'why'.

Many patients leave modern hospitals 'cured' but with little idea of what was wrong with them, what caused it, how to prevent it happening again or how their lifestyle affects their health. In searching for the 'what' it is easy for patients to be seen as 'diseases' and not as people who are 'dis-eased'. With modern sophisticated diagnostic techniques for discovering the 'what', the 'why' is often overlooked, and so the emotional, social and spiritual factors that are important in illness are missed.

Mind–Body Medicine

All illness is psychosomatic. Every sickness has psychological/spiritual factors as well as somatic or physical components. Unfortunately, when the label 'psychosomatic' is used in medical circles, the usual inference is that the patient has a psychological problem and not a 'real' illness. The relationship of the body and mind in illness has been well known from ancient times, but because of tremendous scientific advances in elucidating the physical causes of illness, this link is often overlooked today. Plato[8] wrote in 400 BC:

All diseases of the body proceed from the mind or soul . . . The great error of our day is that physicians separate soul from body. The cure of the part should not be attempted without treatment of the whole.

Wholeness means health of the whole person, not just the body.

THE WELLNESS MODEL

Over the last few years a lot of attention has been given to a more wholistic view of health, which includes the mind and emotions as well as the body. The impetus has come primarily from outside the medical profession, but many doctors and nurses are working within this wider approach now. Dr John Travis MD founded the world's first Wellness Centre in Mill Valley, California, in 1975. His model of the Illness–Wellness continuum is shown in Figure 1.2. It demonstrates the limits of the normal medical or treatment approach. The Wellness Model includes the treatment model but moves beyond it.

Most people spend much of their lives at the 'neutral point', neither unwell nor fully well. We know when we are sick by recognising the symptoms and signs of illness, such as headache, fever and weakness. If symptoms persist, most people will seek help from a medical professional to diagnose the problem and provide treatment. If not, they may proceed towards premature death.

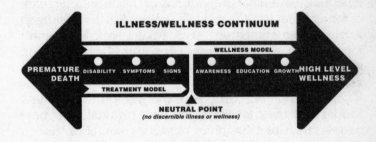

Figure 1.2. The Wellness Model (Dr John Travis)[9]

The treatment model aims to bring people back to the neutral point, where there is no evidence of treatable illness. We are then told that we are well. Someone at the neutral point may be free of overt illness but may be far from well: overweight, smoking heavily, not managing stress properly, sleeping poorly and without healthy relationships.

Moving on from the neutral point starts with *self-*

awareness. This includes understanding how your body works, what your needs are, and how you can achieve wellness. It is an evaluation of your life. The objective is 'high level wellness', which is not a destination but a journey, not a goal but a lifestyle. This process is assisted by *health education*, and there is much more information on health available now than in previous generations. We need an open yet critical mind to sift truth from fantasy, and may require some help from people we trust who are more informed in these areas. However, there is little excuse for ignorance in health matters today.

The next step often involves taking a risk, moving from the known way and trying out new options. It presupposes a *desire to grow*, to discover life and attain high level wellness. One of the reasons people do not move towards wellness is fear of change or failure. Personally, we have grown tired of the clichéd farewell comment that is often used: 'Take care!' After talking to a friend, we sometimes say: 'Take a risk!' We don't mean to go out and break a leg, but 'Try something new. Expand your horizons. Move out of your comfort zone'.

There is a big difference between the Wellness Model and the traditional treatment model. For most people, treatment involves expecting someone else to fix the problem. The *sickness contract* is: 'I have a problem, and you have the knowledge, Doctor, so I'm paying you to fix it.' The *Wellness contract* is: 'I have a problem and I'm prepared to do something about it, but need a little help from others who have more knowledge.' The medical professional then becomes a partner in my healing, not the director.

The key is *responsibility*. Taking responsibility for myself is the start of healing and moving towards physical, emotional and spiritual wholeness. It involves discovering my own needs and finding ways to meet them; being aware of my limitations but also possibilities for growth; learning to ask the right questions, not just waiting for answers. It means becoming an *actor* in life and not merely a reactor. I may require some help in this journey, but I will find the resources I need. It is a process of knowing who I am in my uniqueness, and striving to fully become the person I was created to be.

Life expectancy

Does wellness living increase life expectancy? Our maximum life span appears to be genetically determined, depending on our DNA coding. Healthy living will not alter this, but it will reduce the likelihood of premature death. The major causes of death in the Western world are such things as heart attacks, strokes, emphysema and lung cancer. These conditions are occurring increasingly in younger age groups and are significantly affected by lifestyle factors. Wellness living has the effect of postponing these diseases from mid-life to the brief period before the end of a normal life-span.[10] But whatever effect wellness living has on the quantity of life, it certainly improves the *quality* of life significantly.

Universal model

While this Wellness Model is particularly relevant to *physical* wellbeing, it can also be applied to the other four aspects of wholeness that we are considering. Many people are at the 'neutral point' in those areas too. For example, we may have a reasonable level of *mental* competence but be far below our intellectual capacity. *Emotional* immaturity is common in people who may be well-developed in other areas. Even though comparatively few people are emotionally sick in society, many of us fail to grow emotionally and struggle to handle our emotions well or use them effectively to build the depth of intimacy with others that we desire.

25

Most people have some friends and have found a level of *social* adjustment with which they are reasonably comfortable. However, many of us could improve our communication skills and competence in conflict resolution. There is usually room for growth to become more 'other-centred', sensitive to the needs of others and socially whole. It is also easy to stay at the 'neutral point' *spiritually* and fail to grow in spiritual wholeness. All five aspects of wholeness, physical, mental, emotional, social and spiritual will be explored in subsequent chapters. 'High level wellness' can be attained in all of these areas.

PSYCHOLOGICAL MODELS

There are a number of psychological models which move away from the therapeutic approach of 'fixing people' and emphasise aspects of growth to wholeness:

1) Abraham Maslow propounded the process of *self-actualisation*. By this he referred to the way a personality develops and grows out of neurotic or infantile behaviour and is able to face real problems in life with maturity. He asserts that this concept of growth towards maturity and wholeness is part of being human.

> Man demonstrates in his own nature a pressure toward fuller and fuller Being, more and more perfect actualisation of his humanness, in exactly the same naturalistic, scientific sense that an acorn may be said to be pressing toward being an oak tree . . . Creativeness, spontaneity, selfhood, authenticity, caring for others, being able to love, yearning for the truth are embryonic potentialities belonging to his species-membership, just as much as are his arms and legs, brain and eyes. [11]

Maslow cites much clinical and research data to support this thesis, but admits that his conclusions are based on 'adults who have, so to speak, succeeded. I have little information on the non-successes, the ones who dropped out along the way.'[12] Many of us are aware of times when we have not succeeded. Human nature has potential for growth and goodness but also for failure and depravity. This century has seen unprecedented technological, cultural and philanthropic advances along with displays of greed, exploitation and even genocide. This duality of wanting to do what is good and right and yet doing the opposite, or at least falling below our own standards and expectations, is something which we can all recognise in ourselves.[13] This is a problem that must be faced if we are to move towards wholeness.

2) Psychiatrist Viktor Frankl survived the horrors of Auschwitz and other Nazi concentration camps for several years, and records his experience in his moving book *Man's Search for Meaning*.[14] He observed in other prisoners as well as in himself, that people who had a reason to live or a task waiting for them to fulfil were more apt to survive than those who did not. This same conclusion has been reached by psychiatric investigations into Japanese, North Korean and North Vietnamese prisoner-of-war camps. Frankl claims that 'mental health is based on a certain degree of tension between what one has already achieved and what one still has to accomplish, or the gap between what one is and what one should become.'[15]

His *Logotherapy* is founded on the belief that finding meaning in life is the primary human motivational force. He cites a number of public opinion polls in different countries showing that eighty per cent of people put 'finding a purpose and meaning in life' as their primary goal. This is significant against the backdrop of modern society which is characterised by boredom, where meaning is often sought in pleasure, power, materialism or drugs. Frankl taught that meaning in life is discovered in three different ways, by: (a) Creating work or doing a significant task. (b) Encountering something or someone and learning how to love others. (c) The attitude we have towards suffering. If there is meaning in life, there must also be meaning to suffering and death.[16]

3) Another significant contribution to the development of pyschological health is the *Reality Therapy* of William Glasser.[17] Its emphasis is on helping people take responsibility for themselves in their present and future behaviour. In using this approach with patients in psychiatric institutions, Glasser found that some of them decided they did not need to hide there any more, and they were able to go back into society. Reality therapy focuses on helping individuals understand and accept their gifts and abilities as well as their limitations. Clients are encouraged to make choices. God has created us all with the capacity to choose, and a commitment to take responsibility for ourselves develops maturity. We may need some help to identify and follow through our life goals, but the responsibility is ours.

4) *Rational Emotive Therapy* was developed by Albert Ellis, who asserts that psychological problems are often the result of irrational beliefs and thought patterns.[18]

We interpret every event or thought through the 'grid' of our belief system, which determines the resultant feeling or action. The A-B-C model summarises this. (Fig 1.3)

The following are some examples to illustrate this model:

- It is raining. One person is pleased because her garden needs watering. Another is disappointed because he wanted to go to watch a sports feature, which has been cancelled. Both conclusions (feelings) depended on their value systems (B), not on the rain (A).

- Three people have been insulted. One person responds with violence. Another dismisses it as too trivial to be concerned about. The third person chooses to forgive. Clearly the conclusions (actions) depended on the value systems of the three individuals. Their responses and behaviour depend on 'B' rather than 'A'.

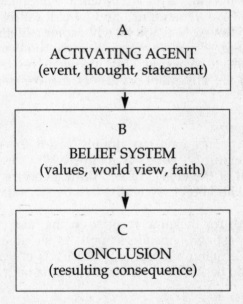

Figure 1.3. The A-B-C model of behaviour

5) *Growth Counselling*. In our counselling work, we have moved over the years from a focus on problems to assisting people discover their potential; from helping solve specific issues to giving them *tools* which enable them to resolve their own difficulties. This is a paradigm shift from rescuing people to working in

partnership with them in their struggle; from helping people to *empowering* them on their journey. The focus is not so much on pathology as on hope; not on the past but on the future. It involves a change of perspective, from seeing people as they are now to seeing them as they could be. It deals with the whole, not just the part.

Howard Clinebell describes growth counselling as having two aspects: firstly, seeing the growth potential within people; then helping them discover growth skills in their inner lives, in their relationships with others and with God.[19] This is a practical expression of the proverb: 'Give a man a fish and he will eat for a day; teach him how to fish and he will eat for a lifetime.'

There are, of course, many other psychotherapeutic approaches to working with people. The five just described are important aspects of the Wellness concept.

In summary:
• Human beings have an inbuilt desire for growth towards maturity, which is hampered by the downward pull of the effects of sin. But this desire can be redeemed and become a reality in a person's life.

• A search for meaning focuses on the future rather than the past and engenders hope. As the nineteenth-century German philosopher, Friedrich Nietzsche, put it: 'He who has a why to live for can bear with almost any how.'

• We need to take responsibility for our own lives in order to be emotionally healthy. This links with the Wellness Model described earlier.

• Developing a true value system is essential for making healthy choices in life. It does not eliminate problems, but provides a sound basis for living.

• Seeking to grow to wholeness ourselves, and encouraging others in this quest, is the best way of contributing to the lives of other people.

These principles are important, but not the whole story. The Judeo–Christian ethic completes the concept of wholeness.

THE JEWISH MODEL

The Hebrew concept of *Shalom*, which Jewish people use as a greeting, encapsulates the idea of wholeness. Literally it means peace, and the greeting is understood as 'Peace be with you', or 'Peace to you'. But the word shalom has a much richer meaning than the absence of conflict. It means peace in the sense of wholeness, health, healing, fullness and harmony. It includes relationships. Shalom implies integration within oneself, and healthy relationships with others and God as well as harmony with nature.[20]

We each have a store of shalom, which God intends us to share with others. It is not a limitless supply, and needs to be replenished daily by drawing on his shalom.[21] But as we give so we receive.[22] After he rose from the dead, Jesus said to his disciples, 'My peace [shalom] I leave with you'.[23] Similarly, his followers are to be agents of his peace in a world that needs shalom so desperately. Peace-making is not a passive process, merely withdrawing from conflict and being an observer. Christians are called to be active peace-makers. Jesus said, 'Happy are those who work for peace, God will call them his children.'[24] Hillel, perhaps the chief Hebrew teacher of that era said, 'Love peace and pursue it'.[25] In other words, if you want shalom, you must not only seek it but live by it. Being an agent of peace should be a defining characteristic of anyone claiming to be a child of God.

There is another Hebrew word, *Sheol*, which is the opposite of shalom. It is used to describe the 'place of shadows'. The ancient Hebrews believed that at death only the shadow of the person survived and descended into Sheol. Shadows do not relate, but slide past each other without confronting or engaging. They have no joy, no purpose, no relationships – simply shadow. Some people choose to live a kind of shadowy existence in this life. We all have a choice between a life of 'sheol' or 'shalom'.[26]

Shalom is to enjoy
Living at peace with God, delighting in him
Living at peace with others, delighting in community
Living at peace with our environment, delighting in
God's world
Living at peace with oneself, delighting in God's gift
to the world – you.

THE CHRISTIAN MODEL

Wholeness is the goal of the Christian life, and this is the clear message of the New Testament.

Jesus came not merely to save souls but to make people whole. He said: 'I have come that they may have life to the full.'[27] He usually started where people were and with the need they presented, whether physical, intellectual, emotional or spiritual. The Greek word *soteria* is used in the New Testament to refer to salvation in the spiritual sense but also to physical 'health', or being 'made whole'.[28] Jesus taught this when he identified the greatest commandment. One day he affirmed an expert in the Jewish law for discovering the way to eternal life:

'Love the Lord your God with all your *heart* and with all your *soul* and with all your *strength* and

32

with all your *mind*'; and, 'Love your *neighbour* as yourself.'

Unfortunately, this lawyer had it right in theory but was sadly lacking in the social action, which prompted Jesus to tell the parable of the good Samaritan.[29]

Jesus was the only human being who was totally whole, in the sense that he was without sin.[30] Even so, it is interesting that Luke described a growth to wholeness in all areas of life in Jesus himself. He writes:

> Jesus grew in *wisdom* [intellectually and emotionally], in *stature* [physically], in *favour with God* [spiritually] and *people* [socially].[31]

As God, Jesus was already perfect and whole; as a human being, he demonstrated a growth in all areas of life, providing a model for us to follow (Fig 1.4).

However, Jesus said: 'Be perfect, therefore, as your heavenly Father is perfect.'[32] This sounds an impossible task, until we understand that the Greek word translated 'perfect' is *telios*, meaning whole. This word has a range of meanings and is variously translated: finished, fulfilled, complete, perfect, full grown, reached its end. So we can appropriately paraphrase this statement as: 'Be perfectly who you are created to be, as your heavenly Father is perfectly who he is.' Jesus is not condemning us here for our obvious imperfections, rather he is encouraging us to grow and develop to our full potential in every area, with God's help.

Paul too saw wholeness as the goal of the Christian life. He writes: 'Until we all reach unity in the faith and in the knowledge of the Son of God and become mature [*telios*], attaining to the whole measure of the fullness of Christ.'[33] We can measure our maturity or wholeness by the degree to which we have become like Christ, who provides us with the standard of wholeness.

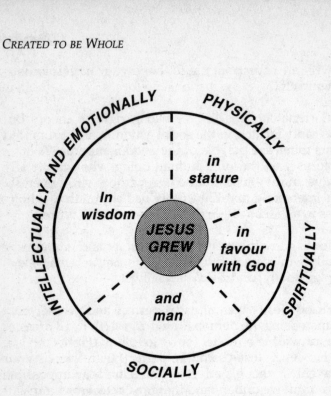

Figure 1.4. Jesus grew in wholeness (Luke 2:52)

Paul said his objective was to 'present everyone perfect [*telios*] in Christ. To this end I labour, struggling with all his energy, which so powerfully works in me. [34] This does not happen suddenly, but is a growth process: 'Stop thinking like children. In regard to evil be as children, but in your thinking be adults.' 'Crave pure spiritual milk, so that by it you may *grow up* in your salvation.' 'Let us leave the elementary teachings about Christ and go on to *maturity*.'[35]

RESPONSIBILITY FOR WHOLENESS

How then do we grow into wholeness? Who is responsible for the development of wholeness within us? It is clearly a shared concern.

• We are all responsible for *our own* growth in wholeness, just as we are responsible for our wellness. Paul wrote:

> Offer your *bodies* as living sacrifices, holy and pleasing to God – this is your *spiritual* act of worship. Do not conform any longer to the pattern of this world, but be transformed by the renewing of your *mind*.[36]

Paul is saying here that my body (representing all that I am) is to be given to God for his service. Am I going to offer him a body that I have neglected and not looked after? My mind is to be renewed and trained in its ability and attitudes.[37] How seriously do I take my responsibility to renew my mind and bring it daily into conformity with the mind of Christ?[38] The whole of Scripture is about how we can develop a spiritual relationship with God, as his Holy Spirit works in our lives. However, God leaves the desire for this with us: 'Come near to God and he will come near to you.'[39] This means that we can be as close to God as we want to be.

• We are also responsible for *each other's* growth to wholeness. Paul took this task very seriously and taught that as members of Christ's body we should have 'equal concern for each other'.[40] We should share one another's struggles and victories, pain and joy.[41]

• *God* has committed himself to the task of bringing us to wholeness: 'being confident of this, that he who began a good work in you will carry it on to completion until the day of Christ Jesus.'[42] What an amazing prospect! This gives meaning to life and something to live for to the end of our days, even after we are able to do or achieve very much. Yet having made this statement that God is ultimately responsible for their wholeness, Paul goes on to reaffirm his personal concern for this to happen: 'It is right to feel this way about all of you, since I have you in my heart.'[43]

Jesus offers us wholeness, not merely a patch-up job on our lives. He once asked a man who had been an invalid for thirty-eight years: 'Do you want to be whole?' This was an offer of physical and spiritual healing, total renewal. The record shows that even though Jesus healed him physically, the man did not want wholeness.[44] We too have this same choice. Our wholeness will be finally seen in the resurrection.[45] 'Then I shall know [myself] fully, even as I am fully known.'[46]

SUMMARY

To grow towards wholeness is our birthright. This process has been sabotaged by sin and our tendency is to choose what is wrong and destructive in life. Wholeness is a journey in which we move towards our potential – physically, intellectually, emotionally, socially and spiritually – in a balanced way. We are each responsible for developing wholeness in ourselves and others, but God is intimately involved in this process too and will complete it in us.

REFLECTIONS AND EXERCISES

1) Reflect on your life, perhaps using your journal if you keep one. What progress are you making towards becoming a whole person? Draw a circle like this and shade in the segments to represent how well you think you have developed in each of the five areas of your life.

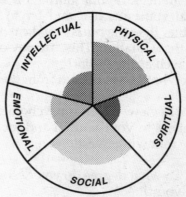

Figure 1.5.

• Discuss this with a friend, partner, or your group (if you belong to one) to obtain objective feedback.

2) Write down specific ways in which you are attempting to grow and develop

a) Physically...

....

b) Intellectually..

....

c) Emotionally..

....

d) Socially...

....

e) Spiritually..

....

• Discuss these in your group and encourage each other with new ideas.

3) Reflect in your journal on some illness or accident that you have had and try to identify all the factors (other than the purely medical ones) which contributed to that situation. This is a way of looking at the 'Why?' as well as the 'What?'

What can you learn from these experiences?

4) Review the five psychological models described. Reflect in your journal and/or discuss in your group the following questions:

a) To what degree do you desire growth to maturity in your life?
b) What gives you meaning for living?
c) Are you taking full responsibility for your life, or blaming circumstances or other people for any of your problems?
d) Try to define your value system or 'world view'.
e) What measures are you taking to work towards wholeness, and are you empowering others close to you to do the same?

5) It would make a useful study to go through the Scripture passages listed in references 17–46, in order to establish a biblical basis for the concept of wholeness.

6) What things diminish your sense of 'shalom'?

What changes could you make to increase 'shalom' in your life?

How are you seeking to bring 'shalom' actively into the lives of other people?

TWO

'ILLTH'

Where is the Life we have lost in living?
T.S. Eliot[1]

In the first chapter we defined what it means to be whole, and described various models of wholeness. None of us have arrived, we are all on a journey of becoming whole. This chapter addresses the major causes of ill health (which we are calling 'illth') and particularly the condition of burnout. There are varying degrees of 'illth'. Some people are merely stuck in their journey, rather like Tony and Jan in Chapter One. Others are far from being whole even though they may not have a definable physical illness. They could be described as 'an illness waiting to happen.' Still others suffer from lifestyle related illnesses, such as high blood pressure, heart attacks, stomach ulcers, ulcerative colitis, anxiety disorders and depression.

CAUSES OF 'ILLTH'

Modern Lifestyle Factors

There are many aspects of modern living which add to the pressures of life and can be significant factors in the development of 'illth'. For example, the emphasis on individualism, achievement, competition and materialism provide goals which for many people are assumed, not chosen. They are often accepted without question as 'the way life is meant to be'. These values can become 'internal drivers' which pressure people into unhealthy lifestyles. Here are three out of many factors which can contribute to the development of 'illth'.

The Tyranny of Time

Time is not absolute. It is an arbitrary mental concept within the breadth of eternity, and it began with the creation of the universe. Before that, time and space as we know it did not exist. However, thinking in a linear time-frame is useful and brings order into our lives. To survive in this modern age we are obliged to structure our lives around clocks and calendars, otherwise we are out of step with the world around us. Efficient use of our time minimises stress, living as we do in a society of 'clock-watchers'. The problem comes when time becomes our master rather than our servant. A life controlled by deadlines is in danger of moving from 'wholth' to 'illth'. The very use of the term 'DEADlines', referring to time pressures, is significant.

Steven Covey and Roger Merill, in their book *First Things First*,[2] draw a helpful distinction between *chronos* (the Greek word for chronological time) and *kairos* (the Greek word for compass). Living by 'chronos-time' means to be controlled by the clock and no portion of time is worth more than any other. It has to do with time management. 'Kairos-time' refers to quality use of time, and the value you derive from it, rather than the amount of time you put into it. This is more related to our goals and direction in life. People who are governed by 'kairos' rather than 'chronos' are more likely to be moving towards wholeness. The struggle between 'the compass' and 'the clock' in our lives results in much discomfort.

The Effects of Change

There have been more changes in our lifetime than in previously recorded history. Change has always been part of developing civilisations. The philosopher Heraclitus said in about 500 BC, 'There is nothing permanent except change.' The difference today is that the *rate* of change is so rapid, and life is changing faster than people are able to adapt.[3] R.D. Laing expressed it: 'We live in a moment of history where change is so speeded up that we begin to see the present only when it is already disappearing.' Scientific knowledge doubles every five years or less. By the time you have learned to use your new computer, a new model is out which supersedes it. All change is stressful, whether good or bad, desired or unplanned. This is particularly true if there is too much change, if it is happening too fast, and especially if it is outside our control. We usually find change harder to cope with as we grow older.

Psychologists Holmes and Rahe in Seattle developed a 'Social Readjustment Rating Scale'[4] which helps people identify the amount of change that they have experienced over the past year or two. Various changes, such as the death of a close family member, or a change of job, were given different ratings expressed in 'Life Change Units'. (The weight or significance of any particular change was estimated by the hundreds of people who did the test. For example, the death of a spouse was given a score of 100, divorce 73.) Researchers found that the higher a person's 'change score' the greater the likelihood that they had recently had or were about to have an illness. Thus, our state of health can often be related to the amount of change currently happening in our lives.

The critical factor is not the amount of change but an individual's *attitude* to change and their ability to cope with it. It has been shown that people who have a positive attitude to change or challenge in their lives are usually illness-free, even though they may be in high-stress jobs.[5] People who see change as an opportunity to grow and are prepared to take risks, seem to cope better with change and without it affecting their health.

The Pressure to Perform

Most people are susceptible to peer pressure, especially as teenagers. Few people like to be different from everyone else, and even non-conforming young people often imitate the behaviour of peers. This human desire to be like others is capitalised on by advertisers in the media to encourage sales. The pressure to conform is seen in the acquiring of status symbols, such as expensive brand-name clothes, the latest model car, or a house in the right area in order to be seen to be successful. The drive for obtaining the wealth for this is often at the expense of a healthy lifestyle and good relationships.

Sometimes this pressure is more subtle. We have seen it frequently in teams, where the leader is a very capable person with a high work output. Others in the team feel obligated to keep up, even without this being stated by the leader. Team members who see themselves inadequate by comparison can burn out trying to keep pace with someone whose gifts are quite different. Comparing myself with others is a destructive and unhelpful activity. 'Each one should test his own actions. Then he can take pride in himself, without comparing himself to somebody else.'[6] Trying to conform to the expectations of others, whether these are expressed overtly or not, leads to distress and limits the quality of life. This happens frequently in society and often in church fellowships. Some of these societal or family pressures can be taken on board by individuals to become internal 'drivers'.

Internal Drivers

Many people are driven by compulsions which define the pattern of their lives. Rather than being in charge of the direction they want to go they are controlled by internal drivers, which they may not have even identified. An important part of growth to wholeness is developing objectivity and self-awareness, in order to determine whether the driving forces in our lives are chosen or are conditioned responses, whether they are healthy or unhealthy.

Some people assume that becoming a Christian means inviting Christ to be the 'Driver' in our lives. I (John) made that assumption originally. Then I discovered that he wanted me to be the driver of my 'car', to negotiate the tight corners and steep hills. Christ offers to be my 'Navigator', my 'Kairos', providing me with motivation and strength if I choose to draw on his resources. The Christian life is a partnership. To use another metaphor: 'Unless the LORD builds the house, its builders labour in vain.'[7] The Lord desires to be the 'Chief Builder' or 'Architect' of our lives, but we are the labourers who do the actual building work.[8]

Here are three common unhealthy influences in life and lead to burnout.

• Workaholism

Workaholics abound in society and suffer from an urge to be always doing something. There are a number of reasons for this compulsion. Many people have seen this pattern demonstrated by their parents or other role models. They experience a constant sense of (false) guilt if they are not working, and when they relax they feel guilty.[9] In psychiatric terminology, the workaholic is referred to as a person with obsessive-compulsive personality traits.[10]

Workaholics often feel under pressure to prove that they are worthwhile people by the amount of work they accomplish. Others overwork because of the pressure to conform to other people's expectations, which we described above. Sometimes these expectations for excessive work are expressed or even demanded by employers, especially if a person is hoping for promotion. Certainly a capacity to work over and above the call of duty is often praised.

Tony had become a workaholic, just as his father had been. He found little in life apart from his work to make him feel worthwhile. He was good at his job and often put in extra hours to catch up on a back-log of work. But his efforts did not seem to be noticed or valued by his manager. He also felt unappreciated at home by his wife Jan and his teenage children. The increasing expenses of a growing family, combined with a determination to prove his significance, drove him to work harder. Workaholism became an addiction for him which was just as real as addiction to food or alcohol.

• People Pleasing

A desire to please others often starts in childhood in an attempt to receive attention or cope with difficult conditions. As the compulsion grows it can become a way of life. Decisions are based not on whether they are right or wrong but on whether they will please others. If we react to people on this basis we start taking responsibility for other's feelings and actions, instead of our own. This makes healthy relationships very difficult and pleasing people becomes an intolerable burden. The word that people-pleasers find hard or almost impossible to say is 'No!' If I cannot say 'No', it means that 'Yes' is merely a knee-jerk reflex and has little value. This does not imply that we should never please others. In fact, pleasing others rather than ourselves is appropriate Christian behaviour,[11] but it should be by choice and not from compulsion. St Paul had some strong words to say about this: 'I am not trying to please you by sweet talk and flattery; no, I am trying to please God. If I were still trying to please men, I could not be Christ's servant'; . . . 'our aim is to please him always in everything we do'.[12]

• Rescuing

In unhealthy relationships, people often fall into three

groups: persecutors, victims and rescuers.[13] This may seem a little cynical but is often true, especially in unhealthy family interactions. Members of the social group may keep switching roles. Some people develop a compulsion to be rescuers. Obviously there are times when rescuing is appropriate and is an expression of true love and compassion. However, 'chronic rescuers' find their fulfilment in life through being needed by others. The result is unhealthy for both the rescuer and the one being rescued, and usually leads to a co-dependent relationship where both need each other for survival.[14] Persistent rescuing devalues and patronises people, inferring that they are incompetent. Becoming a rescuer is a trap for people-helpers and beginner counsellors.

This syndrome has also been described as the 'Messiah complex', a desire to rescue the world. While it is admirable to want to help people and make a difference in our world, this is different from attempting to carry other people's burdens. Christian 'rescuers' need to understand afresh that Jesus is the Messiah, the world's Burden-bearer. This is not our task. We are instructed to 'help to carry one another's burdens', yet at the same time 'everyone should carry his own load'.[15] Sometimes we meet people who are struggling with intolerable burdens and in love we help them. This is appropriate, but it is not our job to take their burden from them, because each one is responsible for his or her own load. A 'rescuer' tends to take responsibility for other people's burdens, and so is in danger of burnout and 'illth'. This has sometimes been called 'compassion fatigue'.

The modern lifestyle factors and internal drivers just described may not seem very significant, but they can cause much stress and constant pressure, leading to disillusionment, despair and depression. We have mentioned only a few of them. Some other internal drivers are: an urge for power and a desire to control

45

others; a search for security through material possessions; and an underlying fear of relationships. We need to address and deal with such things in order to be free to move from 'illth' to 'wholth'.

Another major influence on our health is our personality.

Personality

We are each created with a different and unique personality. Some of our personality and temperament traits are given, others are learned. Drs Meyer Friedman and Ray Rosenman, cardiologists in California, studied the physiological, psychological and personality characteristics of thousands of people.[16] They were able to link a certain type of personality with the likelihood of developing coronary artery disease. People who had what they called a Type-A personality were more than five time as likely to suffer from a heart attack than people with a Type-B personality. Personality factors were shown in extensive studies to be the strongest predictor of whether a person was likely to develop premature atherosclerosis or die from a heart attack.

The Type-A personality is defined by a cluster of characteristics. These people are usually highly competitive, ambitious, achievement-oriented workaholics. They are often aggressive, impatient and in a hurry; hence the term 'hurry sickness' is sometimes applied to this condition. They feel constantly under pressure and attempt many things at once. They usually have a strong sense of responsibility, a high need for recognition, and few non-work interests. A significant characteristic of Type-A people is their tendency to hide their feelings from others, especially anger. They bottle up their feelings. Perhaps the most dominant feature is their speech pattern. They typically speak fast and loud, using emphatic gestures, and tend to interrupt or speak over others. Researchers have clearly linked this speech pattern to a significant rise in blood pressure.[17]

The Type-B personality is the opposite picture. A Type-A person has been described as 'someone who is in a moment by moment struggle against time, other people or both'; and a Type-B person as 'someone who can work without getting angry and relax without feeling guilty'. This is an over-simplification, but it reflects the truth. Clearly, some Type-A traits are helpful and are part of the lifestyle of most successful people. But when they are developed to an extreme degree they become pathological. Researchers found that about fifty per cent of the population in North America were Type-A, forty per cent Type-B and ten per cent demonstrated a mixture of both.

Dr Hans Selye claimed that there are essentially two classes of people: 'Race horses' and 'Turtles'. Race horses are always in a hurry and this equates with Type-A behaviour. Race horses and turtles are born the way they are and cannot change their basic nature. In the same way Type-A and Type-B people generally have those tendencies from birth and cannot change that. However, we are all a combination of 'nature' and 'nurture', but with self-awareness and determination we can modify behaviour and habits that lead to 'illth' rather than 'wholth'.[18]

The important thing is that these *personality characteristics are not fixed*. We can change or at least modify our behaviour, with a consequent move towards wholeness and health. Researchers demonstrated that as people modified their behaviour, this produced measurable physiological changes in the body. For example, most Type-A people had higher than normal blood cholesterol levels. But as they reduced their Type-A behaviour their blood cholesterol level decreased, and this was used in research studies as an indicator of progress. (This is understandable as two thirds of the cholesterol in our blood is made by the body and is not from the diet.) Many things which we are advocating in this book are measures that we can choose to take in order to move from 'illth' to 'wholth' in all areas of our lives.

HUMAN RESPONSE TO STRESS

Understanding Stress

Stress can be defined as:

> *My response* to the pressures (stressors) of life, both external and internal, which make me feel uncomfortable.

Many people think of stress merely as something which happens to them from the outside. Some of our stressors do originate from the world around us (e.g. work pressures, traffic jams, overdue accounts) but the majority of them come from within us. We have identified a number of these already in this chapter. The amount of distress we experience depends largely on our response to our stressors, whether external or internal ones. We may not be able to do much to alter the stressors in our environment but we can do something about our reaction to them. We also have control over those that originate from within our minds.

Professor Selye borrowed the concept of stress from engineering and brought it into medical thinking. His research and writing over about forty years, help us understand the effects of stress on the human body. He differentiated between harmful or unpleasant stress and good or useful stress. The former he called *'distress'* (from Latin: *'dis'* = bad) and the latter he named *'eustress'* (from Greek: *'eu'* = good).[19] Stress and challenge are good for us, and a healthy part of life. In fact, we would not survive without an efficient stress response (the 'Flight/Fight' reaction) which is mediated by our autonomic nervous system. When the 'stress alarm' is triggered, adrenaline is released which increases the heart and breathing rates, tenses the muscles and prepares us for action. Life would be boring without stress and challenge and we need it to motivate us. Also, it is in times of stress and difficulty that we do most of our growing up as people.[20]

Assessing Your Stress Level

Some of the information about the effects of stress can be expressed in graphic form, which is referred to as Yerke's curve. (See Figure 2.1, for our adaptation of this.) The Yerkes-Dobson Law states that: 'Anxiety improves performance until a certain level of arousal has been reached. Beyond that point, performance deteriorates as higher levels of anxiety are attained.' This graph is useful in that it provides a convenient way of identifying and assessing our stress level.

The graph shows something we all experience: as stress increases so our efficiency and performance improves. More demand leads to more performance and it is almost a straight-line relationship. But we all have an *optimum* level of performance, which differs for each of us. If stress continues to increase past this point, our performance starts to drop off. We may be able to work harder and achieve a little more under these circumstances, but we will make more mistakes and become less efficient. Eventually, we reach our *maximum* level of performance (which varies for different people) beyond which we cannot go. This is 'the straw that breaks the camel's back'. The graph now starts to flatten out. If stress increases, or continues at the same high level, our performance drops off significantly. All human beings follow this pattern.

After passing the optimum level of performance, the body reacts by producing symptoms (indicated by little flags). These vary for each person, but common ones are headaches, neck or back pains, indigestion, stomach cramps, diarrhoea, skin rashes, allergies, breathing difficulties, joint pains, sleeplessness and many others. Many people deal with these by taking medication, pain relief or tranquillisers. We have all been taught that there is a pill for every problem. If we are unable to obtain a tranquilliser from the doctor, alcohol, nicotine, caffeine or marijuana are readily available. Millions of people in our society will either try to ignore the irritating symptoms of stress or else rely on a chemical to deal with them.

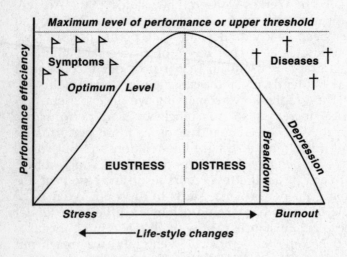

Figure 2.1. Relationship between stress and performance

Distress

If we ignore these messages from our bodies, and continue to live on the inefficient right side of the graph, diseases (indicated by little crosses) will develop.

Repeated physiological changes, resulting from stress that is not managed properly, eventually lead to pathological changes. This is partly due to the depression of the immune system by prolonged stress, as the ratio between the 'helper' and 'suppressor' cells is disturbed.[21] When we are overly tired, we are likely to develop a cold, flu, viral ulcers of the tongue or cold sores on the lips.[22] Eventually, well-known stress-related diseases can develop, such as hypertension, heart attacks, stomach ulcers, ulcerative colitis, rheumatoid arthritis, asthma, and excema.[23]

There is increasing evidence of the contribution of stress in the development of certain cancers. It is acknowledged that many other factors contribute to the genesis of these diseases, but unmanaged stress is a major one. On the other hand, effective life management and working towards high level wellness reduces the likelihood of these diseases, and will certainly assist in their management when they do develop.

People who manage to stay on the left hand side of the graph most of the time remain in 'wholth'. At times, circumstances of life demand that they move beyond their optimum level of performance but they are aware of what is happening and take steps to return to efficient living. They mostly experience 'eustress', and stress works *for* them rather than *against* them. Those who live most of the time on the right hand side of their graph experience 'distress'. Sometimes, hardy individuals manage to live like this for a number of years, especially in their youth, but there is a price to pay in terms of stress-related illness.

The only way to prevent stress from becoming 'distress' in our lives is by changing our lifestyle, moving from 'illth' to 'wholth'. This will prevent burnout and reverse the destructive effects of stress in our lives. Most of this book is devoted to identifying healthy behaviours that lead to wholeness in the physical, intellectual, emotional, social and spiritual areas of life.

Listen to Your Body

One important learning from this graph is that the body develops symptoms (and later on diseases) in response to the distress we ignore. One of the keys to managing stress and developing wholeness is to *listen to your body*. Never waste a good symptom! Apart from the tongue, the rest of the body does not lie. Pain is a friend, not an enemy. Having worked with leprosy patients for many years in Papua New Guinea, we developed a healthy respect for pain. People with leprosy cannot feel pain because the nerves to their hands and feet are damaged by the leprosy bacilli, so their fingers and toes are destroyed through injury and infection.

Without the gift of pain the human body does not survive. This thesis has been profoundly explored by Dr Paul Brand and Philip Yancey in their book, *Pain, the Gift Nobody Wants*. They comment on the obsession of the Western world with pain avoidance. In 1992, for example, 63 million dollars were spent in the United States on pain relief medication.[24]

If we are living constantly on the right hand side of the graph, the body sometimes comes to our rescue by precipitating a 'breakdown'. This may be in the form of a migraine, a backache, an attack of flu or other such minor illness. If we respond to this by taking a day or two off, we quickly come back onto the left side of the graph again and are able to return to work more efficiently. These temporary breakdowns are more likely to occur with Type-B people. Type-A people seldom acknowledge their need of a day off. They see themselves as indispensable, and do not usually permit themselves to be sick unless they are on holiday. In fact, Type-A people often lack self-nurturing skills and are more likely to move down the curve slowly towards burnout and depression. Sometimes they are the last to realise it and others are more likely to notice signs of burnout in them than they are. Burnout and depression follow prolonged, unmanaged stress as night follows day.

BURNOUT

Understanding Burnout

Burnout has been defined as: 'A syndrome of emotional exhaustion, depersonalisation and reduced personal accomplishment.' It is an occupational hazard of professional people, especially those who are involved in 'people-work' such as the care givers in society, social workers, counsellors, pastors and missionaries. We have observed that in certain circles burnout is almost regarded as a status symbol. The inference is: 'If you haven't been burnt out yet, you haven't been working hard enough.'

Burnout follows prolonged 'distress', but essentially it is the consequence of over-use of our physical and emotional resources. It is not so much a sign of weakness as a warning indicator and a protective mechanism. It is the body's way of trying to protect us and prevent worse consequences of an unhealthy lifestyle. If we burn out, we are probably running on the 'wrong fuel'.

Depression is nearly always present in late stages of burnout. It is usually a symptom of the disorder and not an independent condition, though sometimes burnout may reveal an underlying endogenous depression. Depression following intense stress is the consequence of what is known as 'adrenal exhaustion', and this is the body's way of slowing us down in order to allow us to recover. A classic example of this is the story of Elijah with his epic struggle on Mount Carmel followed by his marathon run. He was physically, emotionally and spiritually depleted but recovered with God's gentle treatment of food and sleep.[25]

Burnout usually develops slowly over months or years. The sufferer is unlikely to recognise it before others do. A burnout picture that develops over just a few days is more likely to be clinical depression. Burnout recovery usually takes a significant amount of time, in some cases as long as it took to develop. But the earlier it is identified and steps taken to reverse it, the sooner the person will be healed. The speed of recovery depends on the willingness of the person to acknowledge the problem and make changes in his or her lifestyle.

Causes of Burnout

The causes of burnout are many, and they tend to combine with one another, which makes them hard to deal with. They can be grouped in the following way:

Modern lifestyle factors

Three of these were discussed at the beginning of this chapter: the tyranny of time, effects of rapid changes in our life and the pressure to perform. We can add others, such as: the pace of urban living; the high degree of mobility in society; pressures on family life, loss of the extended family; and the disappearance of spiritual values and standards from our culture. The impact of these things needs to be evaluated, but not much can be done to change them.

Internal 'drivers'

These are even more significant in the development of burnout. We touched on three of them earlier: workaholism, people-pleasing and rescuing. But there are many others, such as a desperate search for security, power, material possessions, status and pleasure. When these desires dominate and drive people's lives, balanced living is unlikely. They are also hard to deal with because change often involves a major shift in a person's world view and value system, and this can be difficult.

Internal 'baggage'

By this we mean things from the past that we tend to carry around with us through life, such as: childhood hurts, rejection, blocked grief, phobias, unforgiveness and bitterness. We will deal with these in more detail in the next chapter when discussing major blocks to wholeness. These issues can be debilitating and lead to burnout, especially when they are buried and not dealt with.

Consider Figure 2.2. We all have a limited amount of energy or capacity to deal with stress. Bucket A represents a person who has 'unfinished business' which he is ignoring and not dealing with. These things consume so much energy (often unconsciously) as he tries to hold them down that there is not much energy left over to deal with the pressures of the day. Bucket B represents a person who has dealt with most of her 'baggage'. There are still some things to work on but she is not ignoring them. Clearly, this person has much more available energy to deal with the pressure of the day, and is less likely to succumb to burnout.

Symptoms of Burnout

The symptoms of burnout are mostly related to our mental, emotional and spiritual life, rather than to our bodies. Sometimes there are physical stress symptoms as well, such as those already described. These warning symptoms are important, but most symptoms of burnout are less specific. We designed a 'Burnout Inventory' some years ago and have used it with hundreds of people. It is a subjective assessment, but if answered honestly can be reasonably accurate in diagnosing the degree of burnout.

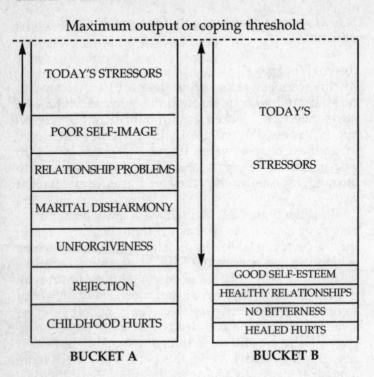

Figure 2.2. The effects of holding on to or dealing with our 'baggage'.

Late Stages in Burnout

When burnout becomes established, the following characteristics are commonly seen in a person's behaviour. These features have been summarised under five headings.[26]

Demoralisation   –   meaning a loss of confidence and awareness of diminishing effectiveness. This may be accompanied by a loss of goals, vision and ideals.

Depersonalisation –	starting to treat oneself and others in an impersonal way. Emotions and reactions to life are blunted.
Detachment	– a 'switching-off' process whereby a person becomes disengaged from people, responsibilities and activities.
Distancing	– avoiding social contacts, and withdrawing from personal relationships, even with family members. Some people become 'loners' at this stage.
Defeatism	– a loss of motivation, drive and joy. There is a sense of hopelessness and 'being beaten by life'.

At this stage, a person may well be suffering from depression, requiring medical help. The goal is to identify the symptoms of burnout much earlier than this. The earlier the diagnosis is made, the quicker will be the recovery.

Prevention and Treatment of Burnout

Burnout is *preventable*

A burnt-out building is no longer of any use, other than perhaps as a relic or a sad reminder of the past. However, it can be restored. Better still, the fire could have been prevented. If people become aware of the potential for burnout in their lifestyle, or they identify early symptoms of burnout, they can make changes that will prevent this process going any further and move towards 'wholth'.

The view is sometimes expressed by Christians that, because our lives are dispensable, therefore we should not be concerned about our bodies or care for our-

BURNOUT INVENTORY TEST

Check through these statements and relate them to what has been happening for you over the past 6–12 months. The emphasis of this test is on identifying *change* in your behaviour, not normal characteristics. Score your answers as follows:

> 0 = You do not experience this, or only occasionally
> 1 = This is true for you frequently, about weekly
> 2 = You experience this most of the time (daily)

	QUESTION	YOUR SCORE
1)	Exhausted and tired	....
2)	Irritable and with a 'short fuse'	....
3)	Having less and less time for people, even family and friends	....
4)	Difficulty in making decisions	....
5)	Difficulty in concentrating	....
6)	Feeling hopeless, like 'Why bother?' or 'Who cares?'	....
7)	Forgetfulness	....
8)	Frequent sleep disturbance, wakefulness, never enough sleep	....
9)	Starting the day feeling unrefreshed	....
10)	Feelings of worthlessness . . . 'I'm a failure'	....
11)	Loss of enthusiasm or enjoyment about your work or life	....
12)	Change in appetite: over-eating or loss of interest in food	....
13)	Overlooking normal duties and responsibilities	....
14)	Feeling unappreciated by others	....
15)	Feeling burdened by responsibilities and pressures	....
16)	Aware of accomplishing less and less in the time available	....
17)	Becoming excessively preoccupied with details	....
18)	Unable to say 'No!'	....
19)	Becoming overly dogmatic, inflexible or 'fussy'	....
20)	Aware that you are driving yourself too hard in your work	....
21)	Becoming cynical or hyper-critical with workmates, friends or family	....
22)	Boredom with work or life in general	....
23)	Loss of a clear perspective on your work or life	....
24)	Feeling out of control in areas of your life	....
25)	Having regular somatic symptoms such as: headache, back ache, chest pain, abdominal cramps or wind, mouth ulcers, diarrhoea, indigestion, skin rash, persistent colds, allergies, sinusitis, accidents . . . or other . . . Score one point for each regular symptom	....
	TOTAL SCORE	_____

(For evaluation of your score, refer to page 62)

selves. Jesus called us to give up our lives in God's service, and said that if we try to save our life we will lose it.[27] This principle is important, but Jesus is talking here about the futility of trying to preserve our lives for selfish personal use. He is not telling us that we should neglect the proper care of ourselves. He described John the Baptist as a 'burning and shining light'.[28] Burning up in God's service is different from burning out. Someone who is burnt out is no longer able to be a 'shining light', and is of little use in the Kingdom of God.[29]

Burnout is reversible

This can only result from making significant lifestyle changes, and moving from 'illth' to 'wholth'. Some of the causes of burnout discussed earlier may be hard to challenge and change at first. A person in the late stages of burnout often requires wise counselling, a lot of support from friends and family and possibly medical help. But the process can be reversed. All aspects of a person's life must be addressed – physical, emotional, intellectual, social and spiritual – in order to bring balance and wholeness. The following is a simple test we have designed for making a start in this process, and identifying areas where changes need to be made.

BURNOUT PREVENTION ASSESSMENT

This is a check list of some important ways to prevent burnout. Score each question with the number that is right for you, between the highest number on the left and 0.

QUESTION	YOUR SCORE
1) Do you have a full day off to do what you like Weekly (5); Mostly (4); Frequently (3); Occasionally (2); Seldom (1); Never (0)	———
2) Do you have time-out for yourself to be alone to be quiet, think, meditate, pray? Daily (6); Most days (5); Frequently (4); Occasionally (3); Seldom (2); Never (0)	———

3) Do you have good vacations (about 3-4 weeks a year)?
   Every year (5); Frequently (4);
   Occasionally (3); Seldom (2); Never (0) .... _____

4) Do you do some aerobic activity for at least
   a half hour at a time?
   3–5 x a week (5); Frequently (3);
   Occasionally (2); Seldom (1); Never (0) .... _____

5) Do you do something for fun, e.g. play a game,
   go to a movie/concert/outing?
   Weekly (4); Monthly (3); Occasionally (2);
   Seldom (1); Never (0) .... _____

6) Do you practise any muscle relaxation or
   slow breathing technique?
   Daily (5); Frequently (4) Occasionally (2);
   Seldom (1); Never (0) .... _____

7) Do you listen to your body messages
   (symptoms/illnesses, etc)?
   Always (3); Mostly (2); Occasionally (1);
   Seldom/Never (0) .... _____

8) If SINGLE: Do you have friends with whom
   you share at a feeling level?
   Regularly (5); Frequently (4); Occasionally (3);
   Seldom (1); Never (0) .... _____

9) If MARRIED (or in relationship), would you
   describe your intimate sharing as happening
   Daily (5); Frequently (4); Occasionally (3);
   Seldom (1); Never (0) .... _____

9) Do you share your stressors/cares/problems
   with others or with God?
   Daily (6); Regularly (5); Frequently (4);
   Occasionally (3) Seldom (2); Never (0)...................... _____

10) How would you describe your ability to
   communicate with others?
   Excellent (5); Fair (4); Average (3); Difficult (2);
   Inadequate (1); Poor (0) .... _____

11) Do you sleep well, at least 7 hours a night?
   Almost every night (3) Frequently (2);
   Occasionally (1); Never (0) .... _____

12) Are you able to say 'No!' to demands when
this is appropriate?
Always (3); Mostly (2); Seldom (1); Never (0) .... ———

13) Do you set realistic goals for your life,
both short and long-term?
Regularly (5); Occasionally (4);
Sometimes (3); Seldom (2); Never (0) .... ———

14) Are you careful to eat a good diet?
Always (4); Mostly (3); Not often (2);
Seldom (1); Eat a lot of 'junk food' (0) .... ———

15) Is your weight appropriate to your height?
Consistently (3); Hard to control (2);
Seldom (1); Over/under weight (0) .... ———

16) How would you describe the amount of
healthy touch you receive from people?
Adequate (3); Frequent (2); Occasional (1);
Seldom (0) .... ———

17) Can you deal with anger without repressing it
or dumping it on others?
Always (4); Mostly (3); Occasionally (2);
Seldom (1); Never (0) .... ———

18) Do you have a good laugh?
Daily (3); Frequently (2); Seldom (1); Never (0) ...... ———

19) Do you engage in a creative hobby
(e.g. gardening, music, photography, a craft etc)?
Weekly (4); Frequently (3); Occasionally (2);
Rarely (1); Never (0) .... ———

20) Do you nurture your self-esteem
(e.g. with self-affirmations)?
Regularly (4); Frequently (3); Occasionally (2);
Seldom (1); Never (0) .... ———

21) Do you practise forgiveness of others
who hurt you?
Always (4); Regularly (3); Occasionally (2);
Rarely (1); Never (0) .... ———

22) Have you dealt with old hurts and 'baggage'
from the past?
All you are aware of (5); Most of it (4);
Still working on it (3); A lot left unfinished (0) .... ———

23) How well do you cope with change?
    See it as an opportunity (3); Struggle with it (2);
    Avoid it (1); Fear it (0) .... _____

24) How much control do you have over your own
    life at present?
    Good control (3); Moderate control (2);
    Little control (1); Out of control (0) .... _____

YOUR TOTAL SCORE _____

Assessing Your Results of the Tests

It is useful to evaluate the results of both tests together:

• *The Burnout Inventory Test* score is interpreted as follows:

1–5   is compatible with good health and no indication of burnout

6–10   is the 'orange' zone, with early indications of impending burnout.

The trend is more easily reversed at this stage, otherwise burnout may follow.

11–20 is the 'red alert' area, suggesting that lifestyle changes are urgently needed, otherwise burnout is inevitable.

21–30 indicates varying degrees of burnout.

30+   Scores of over 30 suggest a person is clinically depressed, or close to it.

• *The Burnout Prevention Assessment* evaluates the resources that you have to prevent or reverse burnout, as follows:

A score of	80	or more indicates that you have excellent resources,
between	70–80	suggests they are reasonably good,
	50–70	barely adequate skills,
less than	50	suggests that changes in your lifestyle are urgently needed.

A low score does not mean that you are suffering from

burnout at present, but that if the pressure is on, you do not have adequate skills to prevent it developing.

More important than the total score is the individual score for each item of the second test. This gives you a measure of how well you are doing in that particular area, and provides a practical worksheet for making changes and developing new skills. The questions cover all fives areas of who we are: physical, intellectual, emotional, social and spiritual. These are some of the ways in which we can not only prevent burnout but grow towards wholeness. Most of them will be dealt with in more detail in subsequent chapters.

SUMMARY

Lack of wholeness ('illth') has many causes. Some of these come from the society in which we live. Others are generated from within us, depending on the kind of people we are, how we learned to respond to life as we were growing up, and whether we hold on to or deal with our emotional 'baggage'. We can seldom change external factors very much, but we can do a lot about the internal ones. A person's internal characteristics, 'drivers' and 'baggage' do more to disrupt 'wholth' than the external factors. One common form of 'illth' is burnout. This is a preventable condition, and can be reversed by making appropriate lifestyle changes.

REFLECTIONS AND EXERCISES

1) How is the *'kairos/chronos'* balance in your life?

Do you feel controlled by the clock constantly, or do you have clear objectives, so that most of the time you do what is important rather than what is urgent? To what degree are you able to say 'No' and 'Yes' appropriately to demands in your life?

- Reflect on these questions in your journal, and/or discuss them in your small group. The conclusions you come to might change your life.

2) What are your *internal 'drivers'*? We all have them. Some are helpful and others are destructive and prevent wholeness. Have a look again at the three described in this chapter: workaholism; people-pleasing and rescuing. Can you identify with any of these, and to what degree do they dominate your life? Do you want to be free from their control, so that you can benefit from their positive aspects but not be driven by them? Are there any other 'drivers' in your life?

- Write about them in your journal or discuss them in your group. Ask God to help you get them into balance in your life. If one or more of them seem to be too difficult to deal with, it could be useful to seek the help of a counselling professional.

3) Are you a *'race-horse' or a 'turtle'*? To what degree are Type-A characteristics strong in your life? Some of these are desirable, but when they are out of balance they can destroy your 'wholth'. Remember, these are basically learned behaviours, so they can be modified to be consistent with healthy living.

4) Consider the graph in Figure 2.1. Where on the curve do you think you are most of the time? What symptoms does your body produce to let you know

that you are past your optimum level? Are you aware of developing any stress-related medical conditions?

- What would help you to stay on the 'eustress' half of the graph?

5) Are you aware of any *'internal baggage'* that you are carrying around, such as: unforgiveness, blocked grief, broken relationships, a sense of rejection or low self-esteem?

- Reflect on these in your journal. They will seriously hinder your wholeness and limit your life if they are not dealt with.

6) What are you doing to care for your *whole person*?

- Use the diagram (Fig. 2.3), and write in what you ARE doing at present to grow in these areas. Then write in another colour the things you WILL do, with God's help, to develop in each area. (Referring to your answers to the Burnout Prevention Assessment test may help you do this more accurately.)

Figure 2.3. Assessing your development as a whole person

## THREE

BLOCKS AND KEYS TO WHOLENESS

Growth is the most obvious evidence of life.

BLOCKS TO WHOLENESS

Small children love to play with building blocks. This develops their creativity and sense of fun, even if they build just for the joy of knocking it all over. The way we learn to play is a metaphor for life. Just as a child may be uncreative with his building blocks, so an adult can lack creativity and vision in working towards wholeness. Life's 'blocks' can be seen as obstructions, or alternatively as material from which we can build our lives. Limited vision is one of these hindrances to growth.

Block 1. Lack of Vision

If building blocks are stacked in front of children they will most likely knock them down. When adults create or meet obstructions they often make excuses, such as: 'I can't see past it'; 'It's too difficult'; 'It seems unnecessary'; 'I'm OK as I am'. So they don't try. These attitudes are typical of people who do not face the challenges of life. They see difficulties as threats rather than opportunities to grow. Lack of vision of life's potential limits us as people. Just as bored children want to be entertained, so as adults we may seek distraction rather than challenge. We can become too absorbed with pleasure or work to see beyond the present.

Jesus talked about people who go down the wide road to destruction, follow the crowd or drift with the tide. He challenged his listeners to choose the narrow road.[1] We inevitably reduce our options when we have an aim in life. People who desire growth to wholeness are focused but not restricted. They have clear goals but do not suffer from 'tunnel vision'. With limited vision we make excuses to avoid change.

Solomon said, 'Where there is no vision, the people perish.'[2] Without goals in life we stagnate. Whole people have a vision of life which is far greater than themselves. They are outward looking without ignoring their inner development. What motivates us and what prevents us from taking on challenges in life? Our modelling is one of the powerful influences. If we see others going forward, achieving and making progress, we are likely to follow their example and set clear goals for ourselves.

Block 2. Our Modelling

If children have no interest in playing with blocks, a parent may try to motivate them by demonstrating how to build such things as towers, bridges, walls or patterns. This can stimulate their creativity. Similarly, in our growth to wholeness we can be inspired by others. The strongest influence in our lives is usually our parents. If our parents and family do not provide a healthy model of wholeness for us, we must look elsewhere for other options. They did their best, but were probably struggling with the modelling they had received themselves while growing up. Reviewing our modelling need not be a blaming exercise, but a way of understanding ourselves better.

We sometimes comment to our own adult children that their lives seem filled with busyness and drive. They respond with: 'Who do you think we are copying?'

And we thought we had been balanced models for them! Hopefully, we are providing a better example in later life, but the most lasting modelling is absorbed in early childhood. Jesus had severe criticism for those who deliberately caused others to stumble, especially the 'little ones'.[3] Parents can be a stumbling block to their children however unintentionally.

Block 3. Childhood Hurts

In the last chapter we described how people carry 'internal baggage' with them through life. This hinders progress and can lead to burnout. It stands to reason, that if I have a heavy load to carry I will not move on as freely as someone who is less encumbered.

Where does our 'baggage' come from? It is often the result of hurts accumulated in childhood, such as abuse (emotional, physical or sexual), neglect, rejection, negative 'parent messages', shame, guilt, loss and fear. These are real hurts. Other hurts (which can feel just as real) come from *misinterpretations* that the child makes. Children are good observers but bad interpreters. Their perception of situations that were intended for their good can sometimes be interpreted by them as hurtful. Whether the hurt is real or perceived it is absorbed by the child, who at an early age is usually not able to deal with it effectively.

Not long ago, one of our adult children told me (Agnes): 'A strong memory from childhood that I have of you, Mum, is of your back.' This astonished me initially, until I realised that it portrayed my busyness as a mother caring for four pre-schoolers who had to take their turn for my attention. I am so glad that she was able to share this memory with me, as it allowed us to talk it through and also to reflect on the many close and happy times we had together in those days.

Hurts are often pushed down inside because they are too painful to face. This kind of 'baggage' will hinder growth to wholeness. In Figure 2.2, Bucket A illustrates a life that is too full of what has been internalised earlier, leaving little room or energy for other things.

Childhood memories of hurts are absorbed but often 'forgotten' and buried in the subconsious. Unless they are dealt with they will stunt growth. These hurts can be reinforced later by other experiences and become 'padlocks' which restrict us. We have all been sinned against as much as we ourselves have sinned. To grow towards wholeness, we need to be aware of things that are perhaps unconsciously holding us back. Discovering them is the first step to unblocking the process.

Block 4. Low Self-Esteem

Another major block preventing growth to wholeness is believing I am of little or no value. This means seeing myself negatively, thinking I am worthless or even hating myself. The painful preoccupation that this view of self brings inhibits personal growth. I can become so absorbed in my self-rejection that I am at an impasse. This prevents me from moving on to discover my potential and the purpose for which I was created. So if low self-esteem is blocking my growth, I need to recognise this and take steps to overcome and change this perception.

In our counselling practice, we have come across many individuals who are stuck in this way of thinking about themselves. Change is possible and we have seen dramatic transformation in the lives of people who have worked through this issue. In our previous book, *Created for Love*,[4] we deal with the process of growing in self-esteem. We describe there how to move from thinking of yourself as worthless to valuing yourself; from hating to loving yourself. While friends and others can help, we need to let God in on the process so that we come to see ourselves as he does. It is a long journey, but as the Chinese proverb says: 'A journey of a thousand miles begins with the first step.'[5]

Block 5. Emotional Immaturity

Maturity results from growing in every area of life including our emotions. Personal growth needs the full awareness of our emotions and the ability to deal with them appropriately. This is where many people are blocked, having been taught to ignore, deny or repress them. In our society, emotions have bad press. Being 'emotional' is a term often used to describe someone who is neurotic or out of control, unable to handle life or deal with difficult situations. Emotions are an important part of who we are, and if we are unaware of them we do not yet know our true selves.

People with low self-esteem have an urge to achieve and 'do' in order to prove that they are OK. A total focus in life on *doing* to the neglect of *being*, on achievement to the detriment of who we are becoming, results in unbalanced development. To 'be' involves discovering my unique self, especially my feelings which are individually mine. If I do not like the way I feel, I may repress or ignore these feelings. Facing these negative feelings can be hard, but the effort is worthwhile. Growing emotionally is a lifelong journey. We explore this further in Chapter Six.

Block 6. Unforgiveness and Bitterness

In 1989, we were visiting Beijing, at the time of the student protests in Tiananmen Square. Travelling around the city was difficult. Often we came face to face with crowds of people filling the streets. This sort of road block would clear in time, but one day we came to a complete halt. Two buses had been overturned right across the road which prevented our vehicle from proceeding any further. It was a massive obstruction which would have required heavy machinery to clear it.

We sometimes need help from other people in clearing away our blocks to wholeness. The twin obstacles of unforgiveness and bitterness are like these two over-turned buses. They can eat away at us, just as rust will inevitably set in on wrecked vehicles. It is possible to be so absorbed with 'PMS' (poor me syndrome) that we wallow in self-pity and continually blame others.

We all have an instinctive desire to get even or to pay back. If we cannot do this, we may nurse the hurt and want revenge. It seems fair that the one who caused the hurt should pay. Revenge turns to hatred which then becomes bitterness. It has been shown that bitterness inhibits our immune system, leaving us prone to illness as well as emotional damage.

Bitterness is like a plaster cast which sets rigid. We become hemmed in and unable to move along in our growth to wholeness. At the same time the bitterness grows and sends down long, strangling roots which go so deep that they will be hard to pull out.[6] How can we be free from bitterness when it has such a stranglehold? We address this later in this chapter under the 'key' of forgiveness.

Block 7. Grief and Loss

Sometimes the block to emotional growth is unre-solved grief. People often say, 'Time will heal.' *Time by itself does not heal grief*, although healing takes time. The grieving person must work through their emotions of denial, anger and self-pity. If the loss occurred in child-hood, it is more difficult to deal with the resulting grief and pain. Children often cope by burying their feelings internally, hoping they will go away.

Shirley was the youngest of four children. She knew her mother was not well, but was not told that she might die; the family considered that she was too young to understand. So, although Shirley suspected that something was not right, she was unprepared for her mother's death. The secrecy added to her confu-sion. The rest of her family grieved, but she was shut out of the process. She was overlooked by the others, possibly because of their own intense grief.

I (Agnes) met Shirley when she was in her early twenties. She was sometimes suicidal and felt abandoned by her family, friends and God. Only when she went back to the memories of her childhood experience of grief was she able to start working on her buried emotions and do some unblocking to free herself. She had been holding down the pain for so long that it had become a way of life. As Shirley courageously faced her past hurts she started on the road to recovery. In her imagination, she returned to her childhood and relived the hurts of rejection, loneliness, abandonment and fear. Many tears were shed during this process, but as the depression lifted, Shirley became free to move on to wholeness. She was now able to deal with subsequent losses in her life.

The first loss/death is not forgotten but 'continues to sit on our shoulders; guiding our response to future separations, until we put it to rest. When you lose a parent early, you develop increased sensitivity to later loss. The answer isn't to bury that early experience but to understand it, accept it, and deal with it so as to prevent it from interfering with your adult life.'[7] Later losses can then be faced as they come.

Many people have unresolved grief in their lives. Even if our experience is not as traumatic as Shirley's, any loss results in grief which must be acknowledged and dealt with. Examples of loss are: denied opportunities, loss of health, youth, friendships, job, marriage break-up, or even children leaving home. Denial of these losses and failure to mourn them blocks the grief process. Jesus said, 'Happy are those who mourn; God will comfort them!'[8]

Block 8. Fear of Change

The unknown can be scary. Sometimes the discomfort of familiar things that we do not like seems preferable to risking change, even to something better. Most people resist change. When fear of change absorbs our thinking, it may lead to destructive phobias which can be even harder to break. Fear immobilises us like an old car with flat tyres, wheels that will not turn, rusty gears and a dead battery.

Fear of change can lead to a sense of hopelessness, but this is only in our minds. While the spirit of a person is alive there is hope of regeneration, just as old cars can be restored. The possibility of change is a spark that needs to be fanned to a flame. Some common excuses for avoiding change are: 'I don't like new challenges'; 'It's too hard'; 'I won't be able to keep it up'; 'Better not to try than fail'. So I hold back. Fear of failure can stop me from taking risks or making changes. I will not seek change without motivation, a determination to grow and opening myself to new possibilities and challenges.

We need to take *responsibility* for our growth to wholeness, but there is help along the way, not the least being the strength of God's love and power in our lives. Friends can inspire and encourage us, and working through difficulties with a skilled counsellor can be liberating.

Having looked at blocks to wholeness, we now consider some of the keys to becoming a whole person.

KEYS TO WHOLENESS

Growth to wholeness does not happen automatically, it requires our active participation. Like a key placed in a lock, we must turn the key, push open the door and explore where this leads. Here are some of the keys to becoming whole:

Key 1. Developing a Wider Vision

Enlarging my vision means to focus on things outside myself, looking towards other possibilities in life.

73

Instead of being stuck in a mould and fixed in my thinking I become willing to make changes. Often a crisis will provide this motivation, broaden our horizons and help us to discover other options.

On leaving school, I (Agnes) was told that I had a serious thyroid problem. I wanted to ignore it, but advice from the doctor was to rest and become less active. I was later ordered to have complete bed rest. My whole being resisted this, and it went right against what I wanted in life as a seventeen-year-old. After the initial frustration, I realised that this was a gift, providing a wonderful opportunity to read all those books which I had often looked at on my parents' bookshelves, but had never opened. So, while resting my body, my mind devoured a wide range of books, particularly biographies.

This was the challenge I needed in order to face my own undetermined future and help me set some goals. Looking back, I am grateful that I used that crisis as an opportunity to grow instead of wasting those weeks of enforced rest. I was a shy teenager, but reading about others who had achieved in life gave me courage to take some risks myself, once I had recovered from the illness.

At any age or stage of life we need inspiration to grow and determination to follow it through. This can be triggered by a *healthy discontent* with our lack of personal growth or unfulfilled goals. We see that life holds more for us and have a restlessness to move beyond the superficial. Many individuals experience this around the age of forty in what is often called 'the mid-life crisis'. At this point people are often more open to personal growth, looking at life and its potential with new eyes. The key of vision helps to unlock the door of opportunity.

For me (John) my personal journey of growth started in my late thirties. I was given a book by the Swiss Christian psychiatrist, Paul Tournier, entitled *The*

Meaning of Persons,[9] as I read it, I discovered how little I knew about myself or what life was all about. This gave me the vision and desire to grow and mature in order to become the person I was created to be.

Key 2. Growing in Self-Awareness

Vision is primarily looking outside myself, whereas self-awareness is focusing inwards and discovering who I am becoming. People who lack self-worth are reluctant to look at themselves for fear of what they might discover. It takes courage to change our thinking and reverse a negative view of ourselves. To realise that I am made in God's image and am of great value to him is the basis of a true identity. Growth in self-awareness means finding out who I am in all aspects of my being:

- Physically — discovering how my body functions and reacts (see Chapter Four)
- Intellectually — understanding my thoughts and belief system (Chapter Five)
- Emotionally — being aware of, accepting and using feelings (Chapter Six)
- Socially — relating in healthy ways to others (Chapter Seven)
- Spiritually — responding to God (Chapter Eight)

Key 3. The Courage to Take Risks

Some people find risk-taking more difficult than others and are afraid to leave their 'comfort zones'.[10] Courage is determination to do what is right in spite of fear. None of the blocks to wholeness that have been mentioned can be moved without using this key. As our vision enlarges, we will be confronted with challenges to change inadequate responses and habits that we have developed over the years.

Even when we are aware of the need to change, we mostly find it safer to stay with 'the known way', holding on to those things with which we are familiar. For example, recently we had to upgrade our car and were encouraged to change to one with automatic gears. While impressed with the advantages, we were reluctant at first to relinquish the familiar hand gears. We took a while to become used to the change but now we much prefer the convenience of the new, system.

About twenty years ago, we became frustrated with the limitations of a medical practice which focused only on physical illness. So we decided to re-train in counselling skills in order to have a more wholistic approach to medical care. This was at a time when 'Mind–Body Medicine' was a relatively new approach, and some of our friends doubted if it would work. There is always a risk in moving away from comfort zones. Eventually we set up a medical and counselling agency known as the Christian Care Centre. As other doctors, nurses and psychotherapists joined our team, we were able to provide a service offering 'whole-person care' to the community. It was a risk, but it was based on the conviction that God was leading us. Over the years, many hundreds of people have found help and healing through that Centre.

> I said to the man, who stood at the gate of the
>   years,
> 'Give me a light that I might walk safely into the
>   unknown.'
> And he said, 'Put your hand into the hand of God.
> That will be to you better than a light, and safer
>   than a known way.'[11]

Key 4. Dealing with Past Hurts

We have mentioned childhood hurts as a block to wholeness. Because many of those hurts are buried in the subconscious, dealing with them is a difficult task. To unearth something that is buried takes a great deal of work. The first step in the process is a willingness to go back and bring to mind painful incidents that can be remembered from childhood. Then these hurtful memories can be safely relived in the present, with the insight and 'ego-strength' of one's adult self. It now becomes easier to move from conscious to subconscious memories. This may need the assistance of someone trained in the skill of helping people to recall and deal with memories. Through prayer these painful memories can be healed.

When I (Agnes) was seven years old, my mother was very ill. As a child I felt responsible for the family, although I could not express this then. During her illness, my younger brother and I were staying with an elderly couple who had had little experience with children. I can still recall the loneliness and uncertainty of that period and the burden of looking after my little brother.

Fifty years later, at a training session on prayer for healing of childhood hurts, I became aware that my persistent shoulder and neck tension was associated with that painful childhood memory. I realised that I was still feeling overly responsible for people, especially in my counselling work. After prayer, my neck tension went and I made a conscious decision to stop carrying other people's burdens on my shoulders. My goal as I work with people now is to help them grow as they face their problems.

Past hurts leave us with reminders. What do we do with these? The key is to *re-member*, or 'put together again' those pieces that did not make sense in childhood because our emotions were immature.[12] Our bodies often express physically the things that our subconscious has not dealt with. (This process of 'somatisation of emotions' is described further in the next chapter.) Sometimes buried memories are associated with ways in which we have been physically or emotionally traumatised by others. When this is so, healing of these hurts must eventually include forgiveness.

Key 5. Forgiveness

Forgiveness is the key which unlocks the closed door of resentment and bitterness resulting from unforgiveness. To *for-give* means giving *forth* and giving *up*. I give forth by reaching out to the one who has wronged me, seeking healing. I give up my 'right' to resentment and revenge. This does not excuse the one who has done the wrong. There is still need for reconciliation and restitution if relationships are to be restored, but forgiveness does not depend on reconciliation, or demand it. Forgiveness is a whole new way of living. It is the opposite of getting even, 'an eye for an eye, and a tooth for a tooth'.[13] Wrongs that have been committed cannot be undone. Forgiveness is handing over the right of revenge 'to a higher court'.[14]

David Augsburger in his excellent book on this topic says, 'Forgiveness is not an act, it is a *process*, a series of steps. Forgiveness takes time.'[15] After forgiving someone we may need to repeatedly affirm that decision. When Jesus told us to forgive seventy-seven times,[16] he did not necessarily refer to seventy-seven different offences. To reaffirm your forgiveness daily that number of times would take eleven weeks. We have met many people whose lives have been crippled by unwillingness to forgive, and as a result they carry around bitterness and resentment which limits their growth emotionally and spiritually.

Forgiveness is essentially a *gift*. In a profound way, by forgiving I participate in Jesus' death, when he died to take away the punishment deserved by us all. Forgiveness is costly. It is not merely saying 'I forgive you', but learning to love the offender. This opens the way for reconciliation even if the other party does not want it. Forgiveness must become a way of life. Jesus told us to forgive as we have been forgiven.[17] To experience the forgiveness of God provides the motivation and power to forgive others.

There is a danger of offering to forgive someone *too soon* in a glib, superficial way. We must clearly identify what we are forgiving. On the other hand, forgiveness is still relevant even if those to be forgiven are no longer part of our lives, or perhaps dead. They may not have been aware of their hurtful action. The person who benefits most in this process is the one who forgives. There are ways of offering forgiveness, even when the perpetrator is no longer present.

When I (John) was ten, I was abused by a man that I trusted. He has been dead now for thirty years. As a young person I was able to deal with the hurt fairly well, and do not think that it has seriously bothered me. I have seldom thought of him since. However, a few years ago, I realised that I had never consciously forgiven him, so decided that I would do just that.

One day when I was on my own, I visualised him sitting in a chair. I was able to picture him quite clearly even after all these years. I told him how much he had hurt me by what he had done. I then sat in his chair and tried to express what he might have said back to me. Then I offered him my genuine forgiveness. I also asked God to forgive me for any wrong attitudes I may have harboured. The results surprised me. Firstly, I had a new perception of him. I saw him as a very needy, lonely person and felt sorry for him, even a love for him. Then I experienced a profound sense of relief. I was free of a burden that I had been unaware of carrying. It may not have done him much good, but it certainly benefited me.

Another important but difficult aspect of forgiveness is learning to *forgive ourselves*. Some people who have hurt another badly, with perhaps tragic and lasting consequences, are unable to forgive themselves.

They continue to punish themselves even if the other person has forgiven them, and even after asking God's forgiveness. What they are saying to God in essence is: 'Even though Jesus died to take all the punishment for my sin, I still need to suffer and want to continue punishing myself.' Receiving forgiveness is incomplete until I have forgiven myself.

Forgiving ourselves and others is best done in humility and thankfulness to the One who has forgiven us.

Key 6. Developing Healthy Attitudes

In Chapter Five, we explore mental attitudes that promote wholeness. Attitudes such as open-mindedness, generous thinking and contentment are values that we must develop as they do not come naturally. An important key to wholeness is identifying these healthy attitudes and putting them into practice as part of daily living.

The word 'attitude' is derived from the Latin *aptus* which means fitness. Right attitudes are part of our fitness for life. William James, the famous psychologist of Harvard University, taught that a person's attitudes have a profound influence on their physical health: 'The greatest discovery in our generation is that human beings, by changing the inner attitudes of their minds, can change all the outer aspects of their lives.'[18]

Key 7. Spiritual Awareness

There are several keys that will open doors to wholeness for us. Of the six already mentioned, none of them is sufficient on its own to complete our wholeness. A vital key which is often neglected, but which enables the others to work effectively, is spiritual awareness. Each of us has the potential for this dimension of life.

Sometimes it comes as a spiritual awakening, a new awareness of the inter-connectedness of our beings with each other and with God. We often call God 'our Father'. This acknowledges that we are from him, and as we develop a relationship with him our lives are enriched and empowered. We become centred in him.

St Augustine said: 'You have made us for yourself and our hearts are restless until we find our rest in you.'[19] In focusing on God we do not lose ourselves, but discover our true identity. This is fulfilment and wholeness. If we neglect spiritual growth, there will always be a part of us that is incomplete. We will expand this topic in Chapter Eight.

SUMMARY

Growth to wholeness means not only adding new things to our lives but letting go of blocks that may be hindering our growth. When we become aware of these and deal with them, the blocks themselves can be turned into stepping stones on our journey to maturity. The keys which will open doors to becoming a whole person are not secret insights, but they are available to all of us to use and share with others.

REFLECTIONS AND EXERCISES

1) VISION   Can you define your vision for your life?

• Write out a vision statement. This may take some time. It could be worth having a quiet retreat by yourself for a day or weekend to think and pray this through.

2) SELF-AWARENESS   Identify ways in which you are growing or need to grow in your self-awareness: physically, intellectually, emotionally, socially and spiritually.

• Talk these over with a close friend or in your group, if you are part of one.

3) SELF-ESTEEM   Write in your journal an honest description of how you feel about yourself. Does this indicate a need to grow in your sense of self-worth?

• If so, what steps could you take to change this? Consider seeking help from a skilled counsellor or wise friend.

4) PAST HURTS   Reflect on your life in five-year blocks. Write in your journal a description of these periods, and identify any hurts that occurred during that time.

• Which of these have not been dealt with adequately?
• Talk or pray these through with someone you trust. Some hurts may be very deep or traumatic and could require professional help.

5) GRIEF AND LOSS   Recollect times in your life when you experienced significant losses, such as the death of a loved one, a close friend or even a pet. It may have been the loss of opportunities, hopes, friendships, health or youth or a marriage breakup.

- Acknowledge the significance and reality of these losses.
- Have you been able to work through the grief and move on, or are you stuck in this process? If so, you may need some help.

6) FORGIVENESS

a) Think about a time you forgave someone, or you were forgiven. How did you feel then and now? Have you forgiven yourself? Reflect on this in your journal.

- Reaffirm your forgiveness for that person, or your acceptance of their forgiveness.
- Thank God for the freedom this forgiveness brought and pray for other people who were involved.

b) Is there someone needing your forgiveness?

- Write down exactly what it is you are forgiving.
- If the person is still part of your life, what steps will you take to complete this process?
- If the person has died, or is no longer part of your life, how will you go about forgiving him or her?

PART II

DEVELOPING WHOLENESS

The second section of this book deals with understanding and developing wholeness in the five main areas of our person.

Chapter Four
Physical wholeness means understanding, valuing and developing our bodies with the goal of high level wellness. The focus in this chapter is on several aspects of maintaining optimum physical health: a balanced diet; adequate exercise; sufficient healthy touch; rest and recreation; relaxation skills.

Chapter Five
Intellectual wholeness starts with healthy attitudes. An important skill is effective goal setting, and being able to deal with frustration when our goals are blocked. Increasing control in our lives is vital to managing stress and pressure. Growing in mental wholeness includes the regular practice of 'renewing our minds'.

Chapter Six
Emotional wholeness includes understanding, accepting, owning and learning to control our emotions. To develop emotional maturity we must learn how to process all our feelings, including anger. It means being able to both share and receive feelings as we build close relationships with people and with God.

Chapter Seven
Social wholeness is helped or hindered by our child-hood experiences, as we learn to move from self-centredness to becoming other-centred. This requires a degree of maturity as well as good communication skills. Various cultures have different perspectives on social wholeness. Social factors are vital to our physical and spiritual health, and to the life of the Church.

Chapter Eight
Spiritual wholeness is a missing dimension in the lives of many people, yet we all long for it. It is easy to be diverted by 'false trails' which do not satisfy. We explore a number of disciplines, such as solitude, prayer and meditation which can assist us on our journey into God.

Chapter Nine
A whole person is someone who is mature and bal-anced in all areas of life. Wholeness starts with the individual. It affects our relationships and the community. We experience a joyful celebration of life when we are being transformed and are growing towards our full potential, to become all that God created us to be.

FOUR

PHYSICAL WHOLENESS

The human body is the most wondrous of the world's wonders.
Sophocles[1]

The quest for wholeness starts with our bodies, because we are the most conscious of them. Abraham Maslow pointed out that unless our basic physical needs for food, rest and shelter have been met, it is difficult to focus our attention on other needs such as relationships, self-actualisation, emotional and spiritual growth.[2]

ATTITUDES TO THE BODY

Historical Perspectives

Ever since the time of the early Greek philosophers, the body has been devalued. Plato taught that matter was evil, and because the body is matter it is inherently bad. He believed that the soul or spirit was essentially good, imprisoned in an evil body, waiting for death so that it could be released to experience its full potential. This Platonic dualism strongly influenced early Christian teaching. It subsequently permeated Western culture and still affects attitudes to the body today. At the same time, our culture worships 'the body beautiful', with an obsession for good looks and the perfect figure.[3] Physical wholeness starts with a healthy, balanced attitude to our bodies.

Our bodies are amazing. Three thousand years ago, David acknowledged both his Creator and the beauty of the body when he wrote: 'For all these mysteries I thank you: for the wonder of myself, for the wonder of your works.'[4] The literal Hebrew translation can be rendered: 'I thank you, Lord, that I am wonderful.' Modern medical research increasingly confirms the truth of this statement, as the incredible complexity of the human body is unravelled.

Physiological Perspectives

The adult human body contains approximately 60 trillion cells (60×10^{18}), all derived from an original male and female pair of cells. Their chromosomes combine to produce a unique individual who is different from every other person in the world. The DNA (genetic material in the chromosomes) contains billions of pieces of information which enable the new cells to differentiate into a great variety of tissues with different functions, such as muscle, brain, heart and intestines. The body is constantly repairing and replacing itself from food ingested. Recent advances in quantum physics have shown that the atoms of which the cells are composed are constantly being broken down and replaced. For example, the skin replaces itself once a month, the liver every six weeks and the skeleton every three months.[5]

Each individual organ is incredibly complex. As you read these words, your brain is sorting out about one billion messages per second received from 127 million light receptors in your eyes which form an accurate picture of what you are reading. As this image changes all the time, the visual purple and other chemicals involved in this process are constantly being replaced as the picture alters. The brain has to process billions of messages at once, not only from your eyes, but also from your environment and internal organs. At the same time your digestive system is absorbing the last meal, supplying your body with energy and nutrients.

Your lungs are providing oxygen from the atmosphere, which is picked up by the red cells of the blood and transported to every part of the body. There are at least five million of these red corpuscles in each drop of blood about the size of this letter 'O'. To make this happen, the heart pumps 9,000 litres of blood around 90,000 kilometres of blood vessels each day. Your efficient immune system is constantly fighting the inroads of disease-producing viruses, bacteria, toxins and radiation. All of this and much more is happening automatically without you having to think about it.

The body is capable of far more than just maintaining itself. The muscles can be trained to perform feats of balance and precision such as those displayed by skilled gymnasts and musicians. Human creativity produced by the combination of the mind and body continues to reach new levels. However, few people exploit the potential of their bodies or their minds to the full.

Biblical Perspectives

The body is given great respect in Scripture. We were created by God in his image and he pronounced his work to be 'very good'.[6] God, in Christ, took on himself a human body.[7] 'The incarnation is God's ultimate endorsement of the physical body.'[8] The Hebrew concept of the body was different from that of the Greeks, who considered that the body was apart from and inferior to the soul. The biblical understanding is that God created the body first, then 'breathed into his nostrils the breath of life; and man *became* a living soul.'[9] Thus a human being is a psycho-physical unity, an 'animated body, not an incarcerated soul'.[10]

In the New Testament, the two main Greek words translated as body are *soma* and *sarx*. The former refers to our physical body. *Sarx* also means our physical body, but Paul used it in a special sense to refer to our old, sinful nature or 'flesh'.[11] The body on the other hand is for the Lord and to glorify him, but the 'flesh' cannot do that.[12] The body can be transformed and is the dwelling place of the Holy Spirit.[13] It is in our bodies that we can serve God as 'instruments of righteousness', whereas our 'flesh' does not.[14] 'While *sarx* stands for man, in the solidarity of creation, in his distance from God; *soma* stands for man in the solidarity of creation, as made for God.'[15]

This is a very brief overview of biblical teaching on the body. Clearly, in God's sight our bodies are important, and it is our responsibility to care for them. This does not mean that we should pamper them or give in to them. They are to be controlled,[16] but also respected and honoured as priceless gifts from God to be used for his honour and glory. Scripture does not envisage a separation of the body and soul, either in this life or in that to come. Our resurrected bodies will be different, or 'spiritual', but will be recognisable, just as Christ's body was to his followers.[17]

Healthy sexual identity is an important part of physical and emotional wholeness. Because men and women together reflect the image of God, our sexuality is also derived from him/her. God is the source of both our maleness and femaleness. Our sexual nature is good and holy and something to be enjoyed. It is to be respected and used in a way that honours God, especially in our relationships.

Living in Harmony with Your Body

For physical wholeness and high-level wellness it is necessary to develop our *self-awareness*. (See Figure 1.2.) This includes some understanding of how the human body works, but more especially by discovering the peculiarities of one's own body. Taking notice of pain and other distress signals that your body gives you, and learning to interpret them correctly is an important skill. We referred to 'listening to your body' in Chapter Two. Many people, especially men, have been taught to ignore these symptoms, or treat them as no more than insignificant irritations . . . 'Big boys don't cry.' Others have learned to rely on chemicals to remove symptoms, before they have found out what the symptoms mean. These drugs range from prescribed and over-the-counter items to alcohol and illicit drugs.

The truth is, your body is your best friend. Hippocrates, the 'father of medicine' taught: 'Your body is the best physician you will ever find.'[18] It is not possible to be physically whole without having a healthy respect for your body, working in partnership with it rather than against it. This is all the more significant for Christians who believe that their bodies are 'temples of the Holy Spirit', through which they can honour God.

DEVELOPING AND MAINTAINING PHYSICAL WHOLENESS

Many books have been written on this topic. We will touch on five important ways of maintaining physical 'wholth': diet, exercise, touch, rest and relaxation.

1) Nutrition

We are what we eat. The world produces an amazing range of good foods. There are no bad foods, only bad eating habits, such as a poor balance in the range of foods in the diet; faulty cooking procedures; eating too much, too little or too fast.

Contamination of Food and Water
Many foods have been contaminated by chemicals before we eat them, either at the growing stage or dur-

ing processing and packaging. Common *food additives* in processed foods are colouring agents (mostly tars such as tartrazine, sunset yellow and amaranth) which have a proven relationship to allergies and hyper-activity in some children. Many flavouring agents are added to foods, such as salt, sugar, saccharine and monosodium glutamate. Modifying agents are used to bleach, mature, emulsify, stabilise, thicken, preserve and provide anti-oxidising or anti-bacterial effects.

The average person in the West ingests about two kilos of food additives each year. Many of them are harmless, or are detoxified by the liver and eliminated through the urine and faeces. Others are absorbed and can be detrimental to health, especially if the body's immune defences are low. It is not easy to reduce our intake of these additives in the Western urban world, but organically-grown foods are more readily available today, and most packaged foods list the additives used in their processing in small print on the package. So we do have some choice.

Another source of unwanted pollution of our diet is *tap water*. At least 750 different contaminants have been found in tap water, including minerals such as lead, arsenic, iron, aluminium, asbestos and copper. Herbicides and pesticides as well as harmful bacteria, fungi and giardia cysts are frequently detected in drinking water. The water supplies of many cities are relatively good, but others are not safe. Home filters are readily available today and well worth the investment if you want water that tastes better and is free of most contamination. In parts of the world where the water supply is unsafe, it is essential to boil the water to eliminate bacterial and parasitic infections, and boiling will precipitate much of the inorganic material as well.

Why We Eat
The main reasons for eating should be if the body tells us we are *hungry*, or we need more energy. However,

many people eat at set times controlled by a schedule, whether they are hungry or not. The lifestyle of others is such that they are too busy to eat when they are hungry. There are a number of other significant reasons for eating.

Eating times are important in many cultures for *social bonding* and to strengthen friendships.

Consuming food provides *enjoyment*. In fact, a good meal releases endorphins which give a pleasurable sensation to the whole body. Herein lies a trap. People experiencing emotional tension, frustration or relationship breakdown often turn to food for comfort. Eating soothes us, because it triggers early memories of the comfort provided by warm milk in babyhood, or lollies in childhood. The danger is that eating for emotional comfort, which often happens *between meals*, can put on unwanted weight. Insulating the emotions with food leads to insulating the body with fat. We should eat to live, not live to eat.

Because eating is physically pleasurable and psychologically soothing, we are all tempted to eat more than we need for healthy living. There is an optimum weight-for-height scale, which has been carefully determined and can be obtained from simple charts. See Figure 4.1. For example, the healthy weight range for a man or woman of five foot ten (177 cm) is between ten and twelve-and-a-half stone (64–80 kg). This is quite a wide range, which allows for genetic factors and differences in body build. If people of that height weigh more than 80 kg, they are overweight, and if more than 95 kg would be defined as obese. The further we move away from our optimum weight, the more we shift from 'wholth' to 'illth'. It is sometimes called 'over-consumption malnutrition'. Excess body fat, rather than weight per se, relates more accurately to the morbidity and mortality risks of overweight.[19]

The Health Risks of Overweight

Nearly every health study done in the last decade mentions being overweight as a major health risk. The main consequences are a predisposition to heart disease, cerebro-vascular disease, hypertension, diabetes, arthritis, gall stones and a greater chance of complications with surgery under anaesthesia. Certain cancers have been shown to be linked with obesity. (In males: liver, prostate, colon and rectum; in females: breast, uterus, ovary and cervix.) It has been shown that many of the conditions listed above can be either reversed or improved, when a person returns to their optimum weight and eats a healthy diet.

Losing weight is a concern for many people, for cosmetic as well as health reasons. A weight reduction regime must include a healthy diet which eliminates as much fat and refined sugar as possible, plus moderate exercise. A number of other measures are available to assist weight control. Being severely *underweight* can also be a sign of illness. Suboptimal nutrition can follow prolonged stress, or it may indicate more serious psychological disorders such as anorexia nervosa. Having looked at the reasons why people eat, we need to consider what foods and nutrients comprise a healthy diet.

What We Eat

The main elements of food are carbohydrates, fats, proteins, vitamins, minerals and fibre.

a) *Carbohydrates* make up the bulk of most diets, providing the main source of calories. They are best eaten in the more complex form such as vegetables, pasta and bread rather than in the refined form such as sugar. Vegetables are better eaten raw, or only lightly cooked.

b) *Fats* are mainly found in meat, dairy products, oils

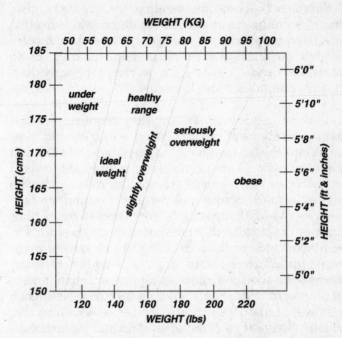

Figure 4.1. Body weight for height chart[20]

and nuts. Vegetable fats (containing unsaturated fatty acids) are better for us than animal fats (containing saturated fatty acids). In a good diet, fats should provide less than 30 per cent of the calories. Fat contains more than twice the number of calories per gram as carbohydrate. A low-fat diet is best, avoiding fried foods. It is good to include 'essential oils' in the diet, such as fish oil, evening primrose, olive and flaxseed oils, which contain Omega 3 and 6 oils. These oils play a significant role in reducing the risk of coronary heart disease.[21] Cooking oils oxidise easily, so need to be fresh, cold-pressed and kept in the fridge. Margarines form trans-fatty acids which are harmful to heart health.

c) *Protein*-rich foods are meat, dairy products, fish, cereals, legumes and nuts. Adequate protein is needed especially in childhood and pregnancy. The recommended daily allowance of protein for men is 55 grams/day and 45 grams for women. Western diets usually contain far more than this.

d) *Vitamins* and *minerals* are also required for the healthy functioning of the body. Fresh fruit and vegetables are the best source of many vitamins, although vitamins A and D are primarily in fatty foods. Two of the main minerals we need are iron (for red blood cells) and calcium (for bones) and these are commonly deficient in the diet, especially for vegetarians. Other important minerals are potassium and magnesium. On the other hand, sodium (in the form of salt) is often over-supplied in Western diets. A number of other minerals are required, such as copper and manganese, but only in trace amounts. There is increasing evidence to show that many people are deficient in vitamins and minerals. Regular addition of vitamin and mineral supplements to the diet can be important in maintaining good health and treating certain diseases.

e) *Fibre*. This ingredient is often low in Western diets, because of the increasing use of refined and processed foods. Dietitians estimate that we consume less than half the amount of fibre that people would have eaten one hundred years ago. Foods rich in fibre are cereals and fresh vegetables, especially root vegetables and the cabbage family. There are two types of fibre: water-soluble (such as oat bran) and insoluble (such as wheat bran). Adequate amounts of both are needed for good health. Insoluble fibre gives bulk to the stool and helps protect against cancer of the colon. Soluble fibre is heart healthy and binds excessive cholesterol in the gut.
A simple guide to healthy eating is summarised in the

well-known 'Food Pyramid' (Fig 4.2). Accurate information on nutrition, based on reputable research, is readily available today. Many books have been written on 'fad diets', which come and go in popularity. Our view is that 'eating smarter' (a balanced diet along with exercise) is more important than following an extreme programme, that may or may not have scientific backing. However, one regime, which seems to have validity (and has had considerable success with cardiac patients) is the Pritikin Programme.[22] It follows the general principles outlined above of a high-complex-carbohydrate/low-fat diet, but restricts clients to only 10 per cent of daily calories as fat, and strictly precludes all added fat, sugar and salt to the food. However, it does not emphasise enough the importance of fruit and vegetables.

f) *Drink.* One common trap is being unaware of the calories consumed in what we drink, in addition to what we eat. The following is a list of common beverages, and approximately the number of calories contained in one 8 oz (230 ml) glass of each.

BEVERAGE	Kilo-calories per 8 oz glass
Soft drink (average)	122
Fruit juice (no added sugar)	75–120
Beer (normal strength alcohol)	70
Lager	85
Whole milk	152
Skimmed milk	94
Thick milk shake	Up to 400
Wine – average	153
– sparkling	173
Spirits	97

Dietary supplements
There is increasing evidence from orthomolecular

research to support the benefits of food supplements to our diet. There are approximately fifty known essential nutrients, including vitamins, minerals, essential fatty acids and amino acids. It used to be thought that providing you are eating 'a healthy balanced diet', you would obtain all the vitamins and other essential nutrients you need. Even if this were true once, it certainly is not so today because of the poor diet of the average person living in industrialised countries, and contamination of the food we eat. For example, the high-speed milling of grains such as wheat, rice and corn results in the reduction or removal of more than twenty nutrients, including essential fatty acids and the majority of minerals and trace elements. So while we strongly recommend taking a multi-nutritional supplement daily,[23] supplements only enhance a healthy diet, they are not a substitute for it.

This is not the place to discuss all the vitamins and food supplements, but we will mention vitamin C. This remarkable vitamin is often diminished in the diet. Even if the body is not specifically deficient in it, high doses of vitamin C have been shown to have therapeutic effects in a number of conditions.[24] Dr Linus Pauling (double recipient of the Nobel Prize) has demonstrated the value of vitamin C in viral diseases such as the common cold and influenza, as well as cancer. It is a powerful antioxidant, which protects from free radical damage in the body[25] and also promotes immune function. It helps the body detoxify environmental pollutants and has been shown to be beneficial in a number of conditions, such as allergies, chronic fatigue syndrome and autoimmune diseases.[26]

How We Eat

Recent studies have shown that people who leave their biggest meal of the day to the evening are more likely to be overweight. Large meals are metabolised better in the middle of the day rather than at the end. It is impor-

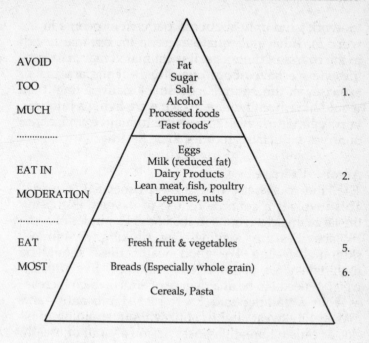

Figure 4.2. The Healthy Food Pyramid

tant to start the day with a modest breakfast. The ideal is three meals a day, possibly with a small mid-morning and mid-afternoon snack as well. This distributes food intake evenly throughout the day, which keeps insulin stabilised at lower levels in the blood stream. The less insulin released, the less fat is stored, which means more fat is available to be used as energy. So it is possible to lose weight, or at least keep it steady, by a redistribution of our food intake without reducing the quantity eaten.

2) Exercise

Most people in the Western world have a lifestyle that is deficient in exercise. The average worker sits down to 'work', and only about ten per cent of people in the work-force have adequate exercise for optimal health in the course of their jobs. It is estimated that in today's lifestyle we have about one-fiftieth of the amount of exercise in the normal course of daily living than would have been required if we were living a hundred years ago. Thus, most of us have to build exercise into our lives artificially in order to be healthy.

Aerobic Exercise
The kind of exercise that is most beneficial is *aerobic*. This involves a continuous use of oxygen, exercising the large muscle groups in the body. Examples of aerobic activities are: jogging, fast walking, swimming, skipping, cycling. For good health, these should be undertaken for about twenty minutes, five times a week. It needs to be at a degree of effort which increases your breathing and heart rate significantly, and makes you sweat slightly, but without straining muscles or causing breathlessness. If you are out of breath, the exercise is no longer aerobic. The goal is to expend at least 2,000 calories per week through aerobic exercise. (This is equivalent to twenty miles of brisk walking or jogging.) A good form of aerobic exercise for people past mid-life is 'wogging' or fast walking. It is beneficial and less likely to damage joints than jogging. It is important to wear quality sports shoes.

Your heart rate is the best guide to the proper degree of effort required. The calculation is based on the simple formula of 220 minus your age. This is the *maximum* heart rate, and should not be exceeded. The *optimum* exercise rate is 70 per cent of the maximum initially, increasing to 85 per cent when fit. For example, the exercise heart rates for a person of forty are:

Maximum heart rate: 220 − 40   = 180

Aerobic exercise rate: 180 x 70%   = 126 (180 x 85%
                                                = 153 when fit)
10-second pulse rate: 126 / 6   = 21 (This figure
     enables you to stop occasionally during the course of
     an exercise workout and estimate your pulse rate
     quickly.)
Note: If you have a history of heart disease, reduce the exercise rate by 10 beats and consult your doctor.

Benefits of Exercise
Aerobic exercise improves health and life expectancy. Some established benefits of exercise are that it:

1) *Assists weight control.* During exercise, the basal metabolic rate (rate at which calories are burned up) is raised 23 per cent, and this increased use of calories continues for about half a day after exercising. Aerobic exercises shifts the body's energy source from sugar to fat. As a result, a person's body composition changes, with less fat and more muscle. Because muscle is heavier than fat, loss of weight through exercise alone is not dramatic and body weight might even increase a little. To lose weight, exercise must be combined with a proper diet.

2) Improves the absorption and utilisation of food.

3) Strengthens the heart. A stronger heart does not have to beat so fast to deliver the same amount of blood around the body. This is why athletes have a slow heart rate.

4) Improves respiration. Exercise improves the breathing, the vital capacity, and the efficiency of the heart–lung circulation.

5) Lowers blood pressure in people with moderate hypertension.

6) Reduces tension and stress and induces a sense of wellbeing. This effect is largely due to the release of

endorphin (a neurotransmitter which has similar euphoric and pain-relieving effects as morphine). The blood level of endorphin is raised 300 per cent after about half an hour of aerobic activity, and its effect lasts about thirty-six hours. Exercise also releases other neurotransmitters, such as serotonin which promotes sleep. Exercise relieves mild depression, and helps a person get in touch with and release emotions such as anger.

Exercise can be done inside a building, and gymnasiums are popular in cities. Good gyms provide expert advice on an appropriate exercise programme for people, in terms of their age and fitness level. There are also benefits in getting away from the house or office and enjoying nature outdoors, especially if there is a park, beach, bush or woodland or a public common within easy reach. Jogging along busy streets, engulfed in car fumes, can be counter-productive.

Sometimes, taking exercise provides a welcome opportunity to be alone; a time to reflect and relax. On the other hand, exercising with a friend or partner can be a relationship building activity. For busy people, making time for exercise is difficult – you will not do it *unless you are convinced of its value* and budget for it in your week. Make it a fun time and something to look forward to. We have included aerobic exercise in our own schedule for the past thirty years, and can vouch for its value to both our health and relationship. Reliable studies have shown that regular aerobic exercise lengthens life, and it most certainly enhances the quality of life.

For Tony and Jan, whose story we told in the opening chapter, the turning point came when they discovered through friends the value of exercise. They lived only five minute's drive from a public walking track, which wound its way through some native bush and up and down cliffs near the harbour. They started by walking together along this track three mornings a week for half an hour. As their fitness increased they began jogging. Tony also joined a gym near his office, and did regular workouts during his lunch breaks. He had to work later some afternoons to make up time, but found that he no longer needed to stop off at the pub on the way home. Jan and Tony looked forward to their exercise together, not only because they felt better as a result, but because these were good times to communicate in a way they had not done before.

3) Touch

We are all born with about 640,000 touch detectors in the skin, which need stimulation.[27] Human beings, along with most animals, have a strong 'skin hunger'. Researchers have demonstrated that touch is the first of the senses to develop in early intra-uterine life, and probably the last to go when dying.[28] Studies in the 1930s showed that children who are deprived of touch fail to thrive physically and mentally and have a high mortality rate.[29] Lack of touch is one of the main factors causing this condition, which is known as Maternal Deprivation Syndrome.

Adults still need touch, but many people (particularly in Western cultures) are touch-deprived, especially the elderly. In other cultures, such as in the Middle East and South Pacific, touch is much more acceptable and is used frequently in social interaction. Virginia Satir claimed that 'we all need twelve hugs a day – four to survive, eight to be normal and twelve to grow'.[30] This may seem a lot to people living on their own, but it is surprising how much touch is possible if we are convinced of its value, even if it is only a friendly hand on the arm. A shoulder massage from a friend can be very refreshing.

Healthy, non-demanding touch dispels loneliness and helps people feel that they belong. It eases tension and lowers stress at times of pressure. It opens the doors to sharing feelings and being real. Even people who grew up in families where there was little touching can discover this valuable part of physical health in later life. Those who live on their own, especially older people, can often benefit from the touch provided by pets.

Healthy and Unhealthy Touch

We believe there is a need for re-education in this matter of touch, especially at a time when the fear of unhealthy touch from physical or sexual abuse abounds. Young children must be warned about this danger; however, children who have experienced a lot of healthy touch from parents and siblings are likely to be healthier physically and emotionally. We should not impose touch on others, who may not want it. I cannot invade your space, but can invite you to invade mine to our mutual benefit. A hug is a perfect gift: one size fits all and there are not many who mind exchanging one. Christians who doubt the importance of touch need only look to their model, Jesus, as touch was very much part of his life.[31] The early Church made frequent use of the 'laying on of hands' for healing the sick, commissioning, imparting the Holy Spirit, and to express fellowship.[32] Touching reduces stress, pain, loneliness and fear. Touching is affirming, nourishing and healing.

4) Rest and Re-creation

For optimum health we require a balance between activity and rest. The expenditure of emotional and physical energy must be offset by adequate time for recuperation and renewal. The Church Fathers used the term *otium sanctum*, or 'holy leisure'. By this they referred to a sense of balance, peace in the midst of activities, the ability to pace ourselves and take time to enjoy beauty.[33] Four practical ways to ensure rest and re-creation in our daily lives are: sleep, proper vacations, daily time out and creative hobbies

Sleep
Human beings are designed to spend about one third of their lives asleep. Researchers have identified the amount of sleep per twenty-four hours needed for health in various age-groups: babies 16–18; preschoolers 12; primary schoolers 10; teenagers 9; adults 7–8 hours. There is considerable variation in the quantity of sleep that adults require. Some people find they can get by regularly with less than seven hours a night. Under pressured circumstances, people can manage for quite some time on less than optimum sleep. They build up a 'sleep-debt' but can catch up again when the pressure is off. However, it has been shown that individuals who regularly have less than four hours sleep a night have a decreased life expectancy.[34] In old age, most people tend to require more sleep.

Sleep disturbance can be caused by anxiety, depression, physical illness or pain. Unresolved issues playing on the subconscious mind can also disturb our sleep. Chronic insomnia needs to be investigated. Medication to induce sleep can be helpful in the short-term, but there is a danger of dependency with long-term use of sleeping tablets. Melatonin is a hormone produced in the pineal gland which regulates the 'body clock'. Its production declines with age, and taking melatonin supplements at night helps some people. Unlike most medications for insomnia, it is not addictive and does not leave a hangover. Melatonin is also helpful in 'jet lag' to restore the body's daily (Circadian) rhythm.

Dreaming is essential to mental health, and adults normally spend twenty per cent or more of their sleep time dreaming. Dreaming appears to reduce emotional tension at an unconscious level. If we are prepared to take notice of our dreams and learn to understand them, they can communicate important information from our subconscious. Dreams are also one of the ways God communicates with us.[35] Some sleeping medications interfere with healthy dream-time sleep. For further comments on dreams, see Chapter Eight.

Vacations

Taking periodic vacations away from our life routine is an important way to maintain optimum health and 're-charge our batteries' for efficient living. It has been argued that a holiday is a luxury only available to the wealthy, and not part of the lifestyle of two thirds of the world. This is probably true, but in some cultures, particularly in the East, even people who are financially secure may not appreciate the value of annual holidays. It is generally considered that three to four weeks of holiday a year is optimal for people living in industrialised societies. Those who neglect this, for whatever reason, usually suffer for it eventually in terms of poor health or reduced efficiency. The maximum benefit of a holiday comes if it is taken in a block of two to three weeks at a time.

Shorter holidays are needed between the longer vacations. Our Maker prescribed one day's break in seven, not just so that we could focus more specifically on our spiritual development and relationship with him, but also for our own good.[36] We ignore this principle to our own detriment. For many Christians, Sunday is their busiest day of the week, which is fine, providing they set aside another day for a complete break.

Daily Time Out

There is also tremendous value in having daily mini-vacations or time-out for yourself, to be alone in order to be quiet, think, meditate or pray. Even ten minutes of this can enable a person to become 'centred' again.

Time alone in silence and solitude brings physical, emotional and spiritual renewal, and ensures balance and perspective in life. Driven people are threatened by taking time out and not doing anything. 'To be idle requires a strong sense of personal identity.'[37] This is explored further in Chapter Eight.

Creative Hobbies

Another important way to bring some balance and re-creation to a busy life is to have a creative hobby. We have been made in the image of God the Creator, so we too have been given the ability to be creative. Some people may have a creative job which largely meets this need, but most people require more creative outlets than their work provides. There are a great number of creative activities, which appeal to different people, such as: music, handcrafts, art, sewing, weaving, pottery, gardening, reading, writing, carpentry; collecting items such as stamps, coins or ceramics. These are just a few of the possibilities. There is a danger that a hobby can sometimes take over a person's life, particularly to the detriment of relationships, and so become counter-productive. But to provide relaxation, a hobby can be beneficial.

5) Relaxation

Much of what has just been described provides good general relaxation. However, there is great value in building *specific relaxation* techniques into one's lifestyle. Relaxation exercises are easy to learn and are a natural physiological counter to the adrenaline stress response. So, instead of being controlled by our bodies when stressed, these skills enable us to be in charge of our body's responses. We have found these skills to be invaluable in our own lives and have taught them to hundreds of people over the years. The two main skills are:

Relaxation breathing

One of the important signs of both stress and relaxation is the way a person breathes. The normal breathing rate for an adult is about fifteen times a minute, or one complete breath every four seconds. When a person is tense, anxious or under stress, the respiratory rate increases up to thirty times a minute or more. It is characterised by rapid, shallow, irregular breathing, involving the upper part of the lungs only. This 'sick' breathing results in poor gaseous exchange (inadequate uptake of oxygen, and accumulation of carbon dioxide). As a consequence, shallow breathers often feel lethargic, 'nervous', and are prone to headaches.

The converse is also true. Deep, diaphragmatic breathing accompanies relaxation. When a baby is asleep (or a dog or cat for that matter) only the abdomen moves in and out, not the upper part of the lungs. It has been observed that by about the age of two, children change from mostly diaphragmatic to upper respiratory breathing. As adults it is possible to re-train ourselves to make full use of lung capacity. In fact, we can use deep breathing to *induce relaxation*.

We can also train ourselves to breathe slowly, at two or three breaths a minute. Doing this periodically during the day can lower the stress level almost back to normal. Many sportspeople, musicians and singers have learned to use this skill. When respiration is deepened and the rate reduced, it induces profound physiological effects. Relaxation lowers the heart rate, blood pressure, metabolic rate and enhances immune function. It significantly reduces the state of tension in the body, especially on breathing out.

Muscle relaxation

This is also a simple technique to learn, but requires a little practice to master the skill so as to be able to use it in tense situations. All it involves is concentrating the mind on various muscles of the body and telling them to relax. In the same way as we can use our muscles automatically to do many things, so we can teach them to relax at will. Relaxation of the body leads to relaxation of the mind. Both of these skills involve the right side of the brain. This can be demonstrated by monitoring the brain activity with an electro-encephalograph during relaxation. The brain-wave pattern changes from being predominantly beta-waves (indicating mainly left brain activity) to *alpha-waves* (which are produced on the right side of the brain). See Chapter Five for further discussion on right and left brain functions.

Even though the relaxation process concentrates on the voluntary muscles of the limbs and body, it induces relaxation on the internal involuntary muscles as well. It also has a calming effect on the mind. Relaxation produces a general calmness of the body and will alleviate symptoms of stress such as headaches, gut pains, general muscle pain and tiredness. The object of relaxation is not sleep, but the release of tension. So the exercise is best done when we are fresh, and it will induce alertness and a sense of wellbeing. A description of how to do these two exercises is in the Appendix.

SUMMARY

A positive attitude to the body will result in physical wholeness through choosing a healthy lifestyle. This includes a proper intake of the right foods and regular aerobic exercise. We also require frequent touch and adequate sleep for health. A balance of work and vacation is important. General relaxation and specific relaxation skills will reduce tension and stress and ensure physical wellbeing.

REFLECTIONS AND EXERCISES

1) Define your ATTITUDE to your body? To what degree do you value and respect it? Do you treat it as your best friend? Is this reflected in the way you care for your body, in terms of what has been discussed in this chapter?

- Write reflections on these questions in your journal or discuss them with a friend, your partner, or in your small group.

2) Review your NUTRITION. A good way to do this is to keep a record of exactly what you eat over one or two weeks. Does it conform to the guidelines described in this chapter? Is your weight appropriate for your height?

- If you are overweight, think of ways to reduce your total food intake. For example, serve smaller portions of food on a smaller plate, or eat one less slice of bread or toast for breakfast.
- Consider the amount of sugar, fat and salt in your diet. Reduce or eliminate the use of these three items in your cooking, food or drinks. Avoid fried foods.
- Be informed about dietary supplements of vitamins and minerals.

3) EXERCISE. How much aerobic exercise do you have each week? If it is less than half an hour, three or four times a week, consider ways of increasing this: join a rambling, jogging or other sports club. Sign up with a gym or health club. Contract with a friend/partner to set aside times for exercising together each week. Buy an exercise machine, or even a skipping rope to use at home. But whatever you decide on, DO IT!

4) TOUCH. Think of ways to increase the amount of

healthy touch you have in your life. Try to have at least twelve hugs a day. Educate members of your church fellowship or social group about the value of hugs, and offer them one when you meet. There will always be some people who are uncomfortable with touch, but hugs are contagious. If you work in an office with someone else, suggest giving each other a shoulder massage once or twice a day. (This may not be appropriate in some cultures.) Couples can learn how to give each other a body and limb massage. Touching is healing.

5) REST AND RELAXATION. Review the balance of work and relaxation in your life.

- Do you have adequate sleep on a regular basis? If not, what changes can you make that might restore you to a healthy sleep pattern?
- How long is your annual vacation, and do you ensure that it happens?
- Do you take one day off a week, even if it has to be two half days? Many parents with young families, for example, do not have a weekly break from their responsibilities. If this is seen as a priority by both partners, creative ways can be found to ensure that both will have some free time each week to do what he or she needs to be refreshed.
- Daily alone times, even if brief, will revitalise a stressful lifestyle.

6) RELAXATION. Relaxation breathing and muscle relaxation techniques are easy to learn. If you do not already use these, try the exercises in the Appendix once or twice a day for three weeks and discover the difference this will make. If you are in a relationship, do it together. Initially, take turns to read out the exercise until you are familiar with the routine.

## FIVE

INTELLECTUAL WHOLENESS

Life is what our thoughts make it.
Marcus Aurelius[1]

Imagine a country without a government, an army without a commander, a computer without a program to drive it. That is how life would be without the mind. The mind is the 'software' that operates the 'hardware'. We do not know where the human mind is located, but it expresses itself chiefly through the brain.

The Amazing Human Brain and Mind Team

The brain is an incredible organ, far surpassing the complexity of the most sophisticated computer. It has been the subject of sustained scientific inquiry for about two centuries, and there is much more to be discovered about its functioning. The brain contains an intricate network of up to 100 billion neurones, or nerve cells,[2] interconnecting with one another via delicate fibres known as dendrites. Each neurone is like a tiny computer in itself, and communicates with other neurones electrochemically across synapses (tiny gaps) between the ends of the dendrites. The brain controls all functions of the body, either directly through the nervous system, via hormones or through the immune system. It is with our brains that we think, plan and make decisions.

While intellectual development and wholeness is

dependent on the functioning of the physical brain, this is not the complete story. Human beings also have a *mind* and *self-awareness*, which appear to operate independently. The mind links the body with the soul or spirit. Canadian neurosurgeon, Wilder Penfield, after performing hundreds of operations and experiments on human brains, came to the conclusion that mind and brain were separate. He observed that even as the brain deteriorates with age, the mind can go on to reach fuller potential.[3]

Estimates vary on whether human beings use only five to twenty per cent of their brain capacity. What is certain is that many of us could develop our brains much more than we have already. The intellectual capacity of most individuals is a neglected area of their total wholeness. One mark of a 'fully alive' person is an inquiring and growing mind. An excellent book which explores many aspects of the human mind is *Your Magnificent Mind*, by Gary Collins.[4] This book is well-researched and documented for those who wish to have a deeper understanding of this subject.

One aspect of brain function which is helpful to the understanding of personal wholeness, is the way the left and right hemispheres of the brain operate differently. (See Figure 5.1.) The two halves of the brain are connected by a bundle of fibres (the corpus callosum) so do not operate independently. Understanding the working of the left and right brain began when doctors started using an operation in the 1930s to sever the connections between them in order to treat severe epilepsy. Many studies have since been done on 'split brain' patients and animals to establish the different functions of the two sides of the brain.[5]

Left brain activity is mainly deductive and the right brain is more inductive. It is important to have a balance between these two sets of functions, which are affected by our culture. Western culture and education, with its emphasis on technology, stresses the impor-

LEFT BRAIN	RIGHT BRAIN
•Language, verbal skills, details	
	Spatial concepts, wholes, sets
•Reading, writing, spelling	
•Logic, reasoning	Forms, images
•Linear, vertical, sequential thinking	Symbolism, fantasy, imagination
	Lateral, simultaneous thought
•Mechanical concepts, maths	
•Seeing meaning, abstract thinking	Musical appreciation
	Pattern recognition
•Intuitive, creative	
•Analysis	Intellectual, critical
•Thoughts	Synthesis
•Achieving, competing	Emotions
•Control, mastery	Relaxation

In Summary:

DOING   **BEING**

Figure 5.1. Left and right brain functions contrasted

tance of the left hemisphere's logical, mathematical and language-based skills. By contrast, right brain abilities are developed in Eastern cultures, which are more intuitive and mystical. There is also a gender difference, in that right brain functions are used more readily by women than men, but this may be partly influenced by cultural mores.

While right and left brain functions are well-defined, the brain is an integrated unit, and the two sides work together in harmony. For example, the left side hears the words, whereas the right side appreciates the moral or metaphor of a story and the punch lines of jokes. The left side reads the music score, while the right side determines the pitch and quality of the tones. The left brain assesses facts, while the right brain appears to be more concerned with moral values.[6]

The significance of this in terms of intellectual wholeness is the importance of keeping a *balance*. Albert Einstein[7] taught that imagination (right brain) was more important than reasoning (left brain), and claimed he often experienced an important breakthrough in his work when he was in a relaxed, right-brain state, rather than while thinking logically. Archimedes discovered his famous physics principle when he was relaxing in a hot bath.[8] Tradition has it that Archimedes was so much in his right brain, that he ran down the streets of Athens shouting *'eureka'* ('I've found it') having forgotten to put his clothes on first! Clearly, we need a balance of left and right brain functions.

Creativity and relaxation are right brain functions. We described in the last chapter how a state of tension can be relieved by a short period of relaxation. Mental and physical imbalance results from neglecting the functions of one side of the brain in favour of those of the other. The way to grow in intellectual wholeness is to develop our non-preference areas (the less used side of our brain), not only the skills in which we are more proficient.

MENTAL ATTITUDES THAT PROMOTE WHOLENESS

There are a number of mental attitudes that promote wholeness and healthy living. These values have been expressed by philosophers and religious teachers down through the centuries. Here are some of them:

1) Total involvement in life

This means living life to the full and being totally committed to whatever we do. The Teacher in the book of Ecclesiastes encourages us: 'Whatever your hand finds to do, do it with all your might.'[9] This wholehearted involvement brings a sense of satisfaction, apart from the value of the work done. Paul expresses this in the context of the Christian faith: 'Whatever you do, work at it with all your heart, as working for the Lord, not for men.'[10] As someone has said: 'People who are never carried away, should be.'

2) Generous thinking

Solomon said: 'One man gives freely, yet gains even more; another withholds unduly, but comes to poverty. A generous man will prosper; he who refreshes others will himself be refreshed.'[11] This is a principle of life, as those who live this way will prove. It is an expression of wholehearted involvement in life. 'Develop the habit of giving things away.'[12] Giving is more satisfying than receiving, or clutching on to what we have. Holding our possessions 'on an open palm' frees us from being controlled by them. This makes the difference between owning our possessions or being owned by them. Jesus identified giving as an important principle of healthy living:

> Give and it will be given to you. A good measure, pressed down, shaken together and running over, will be poured into your lap. For with the measure you use, it will be measured to you.[13]

This applies not only to our possessions, but also in our relationships. The more we give to a relationship, particularly in marriage, the more we will receive. Even if

I do not receive back from a relationship all that I would like, I will never be the loser by giving generously.

3) Open-mindedness

A closed mind is a sick mind. Being open-minded does not mean that we should have no values and beliefs, or make no decisions. It refers to being open to *evaluate* our beliefs and being free to adjust them in the light of new insights, or else to reaffirm our original belief if the new information is invalid. A person with an open mind can grow and take risks. When we stop growing mentally, we stop living. When your mind has been stretched by a new idea, it never returns to its original dimension.

Evidence is accumulating to show that older people who keep their minds alert and active with such things as reading, crossword puzzles and playing bridge, are healthier and live longer. Many are doing university studies into their seventies and eighties. Certainly it makes the later years more enjoyable, and older people more interesting to be with.

4) Outward thinking

Preoccupation with myself and my own world cripples full enjoyment of life and limits my development to maturity. Living in a 'world of one' is a sad and lonely place to be. Albert Einstein, one of the most creative intellects in human history, said: 'The tragedy of life is what dies within a man while he lives.' Being open to other people and interested in what they are doing refreshes us, adds joy to life, and is part of healthy living.[14] Exploring new ideas and interests prevents mental stagnation as we grow older. Discovering what *God is doing* in this world (instead of focusing only on what I am doing) keeps my vision alive. 'Where there is no vision, the people perish.'[15]

5) Positive thinking

Emil Coué was probably the first person to popularise the concept of positive thinking, with his famous aphorism: 'Every day and in every way I am becoming better and better.'[16] This was taken up by later authors, who coined the term 'positive mental attitude' (PMA). Clemant Stone built a multi-million-dollar corporation from a financial start of a hundred dollars, and attributes his success to PMA.[17] Norman Vincent Peale wrote a best seller on this topic, *The Power of Positive Thinking*,[18] which has influenced millions of people. The essence of positive thinking is to take an optimistic attitude towards problems, refuse to give in to anxiety or to have a negative view of circumstances. 'Never think of failing, you don't have to!'[19]

There is certainly great value in positive thinking. No athlete would win a contest if she or he visualised failing rather than succeeding. Our 'frame of reference', or the way we view the world, has a big influence on our experience of it.

Two men looked out from prison bars,
One saw mud, the other stars.

Viktor Frankl never lost hope in the future while he suffered in Nazi prison camps. He observed that those prisoners who did give up were doomed.[20] Having a strong hope, a belief that God is in control and that he will answer prayer, are key elements of the Christian faith.[21] Optimism has been shown to be a significant factor in survival after a heart attack, and also in recuperation from surgery, with fewer medical complications.[22] On the other hand, optimism must be balanced by realism; hope must include an honest assessment of the realities of the present.

I (John) am an optimist. I suspect this came from observing a father who had amazing faith and hope as a missionary in China and Mongolia for over forty years, despite ill health, trying circumstances and much personal tragedy. I went to boarding school from the age of seven, and only saw my parents briefly once a year as a young child. Looking back, I realise that I had made an unconscious decision to be positive about the situation and ignore feelings of loneliness. I decided that life was good.

However, there was a price to pay. To maintain this view of life, I repressed my feelings and tended to dismiss problems. Fortunately, I married a realist, who has helped me to find some balance to this overly-positive view of life. Agnes has found it hard at times living with a 'super-optimist'. Our children have told me that sometimes they hesitated to share problems with me for fear that I would only look on the positive side, trivialise the issues and not really listen. Their honest feedback has helped me to keep my optimism in balance, and to listen before offering comments.

One of the most significant statements in all of literature about choosing to think positively, comes from St Paul:

Whatever is true, whatever is noble, whatever is right, whatever is pure, whatever is lovely, whatever is admirable – if anything is excellent or praiseworthy – think about such things.[23]

To be positive is to be enthusiastic. The world needs enthusiasts, in the truest sense. The word 'enthusiasm' comes from the Greek: *en* (in) + *theos* (God) meaning someone who is 'in God', God-filled or inspired by God.

One aspect of positive thinking is *humour*. When humour is missing, life becomes bleak and grey. Humour and mental health go together.[24] Even in situations of poor health or trying circumstances, humour will lighten the load. Solomon said: 'Being cheerful keeps you healthy. It is slow death to be gloomy all the time.'[25] A good laugh releases endorphins in the brain, which result in feelings of relaxation and pleasure. It also makes us take some deep breaths. He who laughs, lasts.

6) Imagination

The process of visualisation and using our imagination creatively enhances the power of our minds. Unfortunately, as adults we tend to lose our vivid childhood imagination. Successful athletes, speakers and entertainers mentally rehearse and visualise their performance in advance. Drawing on the right brain imagination of listeners is an effective way to teach. Jesus used this method almost entirely.[26] The power of the imagination is an under-developed resource for many people. Children are good at it, but adults often fail to be able to think 'outside the box'. 'When faced with two alternatives, always choose the third' (Yiddish proverb).

Imagination can be used for evil as well as for good. The Hebrew word for it is *yetser*, and is used to describe both good and bad human imagination.[27] However, when our imagination is under God's control, the result is peace and harmony: 'You will keep in perfect peace him whose mind [*yetser*] is steadfast, because he trusts in you.'[28]

7) Disciplined thinking

Discipline, self-control and a healthy sense of duty are in short supply today. We start to learn these values in childhood, when we are totally dependent on and controlled by others. One of the important goals of parenting is to encourage children to become *self-controlled*. They will not learn this if they are overly-controlled, nor will they learn it unless they are given proper boundaries and guidelines. This balance is hard to find, as those of us who are parents have discovered. Successful living requires self-control and disciplined thinking. This will help us to become self-motivators, 'actors' rather than 'reactors' in life. The pursuit of excellence is admirable, but there is a danger of becoming overly-disciplined and rigid in our thinking. Perfectionism is a sign of insecurity, not strength. For health, we need to find a balance between self-control and flexibility, self-discipline and spontaneity, having goals but also being able to adjust them appropriately.

8) Contentment

The thesis of this book is how to grow, change and mature in all areas of life. However, contentment with our present situation brings peace and frees us from anxiety. This acceptance need not stop us from wanting to improve ourselves or better the lives of others, but it does eliminate much stress and tension. 'Godliness with contentment is great gain.'[29] A sense of gratitude and appreciation for all that we have is often missing from the thinking of many people, especially in the West.

Contentment is not a gift but is something that we have *to learn*. Paul wrote: 'I have learned to be content whatever the circumstances. I know what it is to be in need, and I know what it is to have plenty. I have learned the secret of being content in any and every situation.'[30] An attitude of discontent results in much unhappiness. However, we need to have a proper balance between contentment and dissatisfaction with the status quo; enjoying what we have and setting goals for something better. 'Happiness is not having what you want, but wanting what you have.'[31]

Research into mental attitudes

In 1980, psychologists at the University of Chicago decided to study people who had stressful and demanding jobs, but whose record showed that they had a low illness rate.[32] What did these 'psychologically hardy' individuals have in common? Of the many factors they checked, three stood out:

a) They all had *a positive attitude towards change and challenge*. They saw change and problems as opportunities for growth, rather than excuses to give up. They were prepared to take some risks. Individuals in the survey who were prone to illness when under stress were those who used what the researchers described as 'self-defeating tactics', such as watching a lot of TV, drinking excessively, using drugs or sleeping too much.

b) *Commitment*. The psychologically healthy group were people who all had an attitude of commitment to everything that they did. They were fully involved in their work, families, community or church.

c) The third characteristic of the healthy group was that they all had a feeling of *being in control.* Even though they could not control their environment, they had a sense of self-control and influence over their lives, jobs and families. The first two factors we have discussed briefly in sections (1) and (5) above, and the third we will look at shortly.

GOAL SETTING

If we aim at nothing we are sure to hit it. Healthy people dream dreams, have ambitions, set goals, and continually seek to expand their horizons.[33] Exploring your daydreams and fantasies by keeping a journal is a good way of sorting out creative possibilities from unrealistic ones. We need realistic, achievable goals. Without proper goal setting, life becomes out of control and filled with unnecessary stress.

Consider Figure 5.2. Effective living starts with goals, but they must be in an *order of priority*. For this to happen there must be planning and organisation. When this cycle functions properly we obtain the most out of life. Applying our minds to set efficient goals for ourselves is part of intellectual wholeness. Logical planning is a left brain activity, but assessing the value of the goal and its priority in our lives involves the right side.

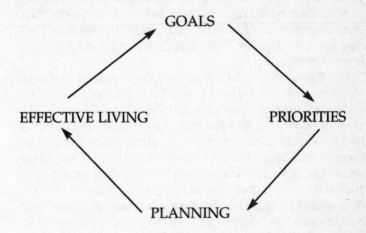

GOALS

EFFECTIVE LIVING   PRIORITIES

PLANNING

Figure 5.2. A model for effective living

Types of Goals

Goals are in two main categories: general life goals and specific, practical targets. Examples of *life goals* would be a career; marriage and parenthood; a determination to put God first in one's thinking; aiming to become a whole person. *Specific goals* are such things as embarking on a course of study to further your career; planning to set aside time each day to nurture your relationship with God, your partner or your children; adjusting your schedule to include regular exercise or relaxation.

Sometimes a major goal seems too formidable, but can be made more manageable if it is broken down into *sub-goals*. These can then be dealt with one at a time. A variant of this is to identify clearly which goals are long-term, medium-term or short-term. Having an overall picture gives pattern and structure to your life for the future. We find that an annual planner sheet is a helpful tool. Ours starts to take shape by about June of the previous year. Then after Christmas we set aside time to survey the coming year in detail, to ensure that our commitments fit in with our overall goals, and that adequate breaks for 'time out', rest and renewal have been planned.

At the other end of the scale is day-to-day planning. We prefer to plan a week at a time, rather than work from day to day. Sunday night is our usual time to do this. We try to ensure that there is a balance to the week of work and rest, time for relating with family or friends and time alone. This means that our two diaries must synchronise. Couples must set their goals and plans *together*, otherwise they finish up operating on two different agendas. Someone has defined marriage as the only human contract where two people agree to permanently interfere with each other's lives. A marriage is hard enough to work out without adding to the confusion by not planning together. A motto that we adopted from the time we became engaged is: 'Hang together or we may hang separately!'

The Goal-Setting Process

Many books have been written on this topic. The steps needed to produce an effective goal can be summarised under the following questions:

What?
The first step is to define the goal. It must be expressed as precisely as possible. To say, 'I want a better relationship with my son', 'I want to be successful', or 'I want to be happy', is too vague. They are desires, not goals. General wishes must be turned into specific tasks for them to become goals. For example, 'I will

attend my son's football game each Saturday, in order to spend time with him', turns the first wish into a goal. Some other questions are needed to explore the 'What?', such as: What resources will I require in terms of time, finance, materials or help from others? Is my goal measurable?

Why?

Why do I want this goal, and how important is it to me? These questions are vital, and to proceed without adequate answers may result in failure. Along with 'Why?', it is equally important to ask:

Where?

Where does this goal fit into my priorities in life? If I am married, is this goal one that *we share* because it is our combined priority? Christians find this question challenging, as they try to discern where their goals fit in with God's plan for their lives. For everyone, this is a vital question. We all have a number of goals, but for most people their goals are in a *'horizontal* order'. This results in stress and discomfort when goals clash. In the example used above of the father going to football on a Saturday with his son, this goal may conflict with his desire to sleep in, play golf or do some work. When goals are in a 'horizontal order', without assigned priority, we tend to do what is the most urgent or the most convenient. But if we have our goals in a *'vertical* order', we are more likely to do what is the most important.

Steven Covey, in his excellent books, *The Seven Habits of Highly Effective People*[34] and *First Things First*,[35] explores this principle in depth. He claims that successful living comes from organising our lives on the basis of *principles* and character, not expediency or slick psychological ways to success. He defines a principle-centred goal as 'doing the right thing, for the right reason, in the right way'.[36] These goals are important, but may not be pressing or urgent, so we may fail to make time for them in our lives. They include such things as relationship building; spending time to find a clear direction and vision (which arises out of a clear personal mission statement); proper planning; nurturing our bodies, minds and souls. Aiming to become a whole person is a principle-centred goal. These things are important, but are not often seen as urgent.

Choosing the right goals and putting them in a vertical order can be costly. When we returned to New Zealand from living in Papua New Guinea, I (John) had a mass of medical and epidemiological data which I had collected over the previous twenty years. I was keen to use this information for a PhD or MD thesis. This seemed a worthy goal, but it would have involved me in one or two years of full-time study. At that time, we had a teenage family, who were struggling to adjust to New Zealand culture again. I realised that they needed a father, not a remote research worker living with them. I found it hard to set aside my dream, but have never regretted the decision to put my family first.

How?

A cluster of important questions follow setting a goal, however carefully devised. The first is, 'How can I evaluate this goal, or how will I know whether it has been achieved?' Only time will tell whether the father and son develop a better relationship, but such things as: 'Do we enjoy being together more?' or 'Do we communicate more?' would be good indicators. Another important question to ask about any goal is, 'How could my goal be sabotaged?' Being pro-active in preventing things that might undermine your goals will save much heartache. Other useful questions are, 'How will this goal affect my family, friends, community, my future?' 'How will I be rewarded (or reward myself) for achieving my goal?'

When?

It is all too possible to have goals that never eventuate. For example, 'transcendental jogging' does not actually produce fitness. 'When will I start on this goal?' and 'When will it be completed?' are vital questions. Without these, the goal may not be achieved.

Frustrated Goals

We all experience the frustration of some of our goals in life. How do we respond to this? Our reactions depend on our maturity. There are several options, which are summarised in Figure 5.3. When our goals are blocked for some reason, we have these choices:

1. We can try again, and might be successful a second or third time.

2. We can change an illusive goal into one that is more realistic. The new goal could prove to be even better than the original one. Alternatively, we might have to choose something that is not quite what we wanted, but satisfactory under the circumstances.

3. We can become frustrated and bitter. This is not a good alternative, but is a choice that some people make when goals are blocked. Bitterness wastes a lot of energy, is destructive, hinders creative thinking and leads to emotional or physical illness. People who turn anger and frustration in on themselves often resort to alcohol, food or drugs for relief. This choice also leads to apathy and depression.

4. We can act it out on others. This means dumping our frustration onto other people, usually those we live or work with. It can come out as blaming statements, bursts of anger, physical or emotional abuse. This leads to breakdown of relationships.

5. We can see the blocking of our goals as opportunities to grow and mature as people. This is an application of acceptance, described earlier in the chapter. It does not mean capitulation or stoical resignation to life's difficulties, but seeing them as things which can

help us grow in character.[37]

Let's see how some of this affected Tony and Jan. Tony attended a goal-setting workshop in connection with his job. He had anticipated that this might improve his efficiency at work, but had not realised how it could impact his home life too. He and Jan stayed in a motel at a beach resort one weekend when their children were at a school camp. Tony shared what he had learned, and they spent time reviewing their goals as a couple. They realised that they had been aiming in different directions rather than working together in the last few years.

Tony apologised for the times he had dumped his frustration and anger on Jan, and she acknowledged ways in which she had deliberately sabotaged his ideas in order to pay him back. This brought some relief and healing. They determined to plan their goals together on a regular basis in the future, and also try to involve their children in setting family goals.

CONTROL

One of the main factors affecting the amount of stress we experience, and consequently our quality of wholeness, is the degree of control we have over our lives. This does not refer to controlling people or our environment, but to the control we have over *ourselves, our lives and our work*. The amount of control we have in life is largely a function of our intellectual ability to think creatively, make wise choices, plan goals and set appropriate boundaries in our relationships.

Control and Demand

The dynamic interaction between control and demand is shown in Figure 5.4. We can be in four separate states, depending on the extent of pressure and stress we experience, and the amount of control we have over our lives.

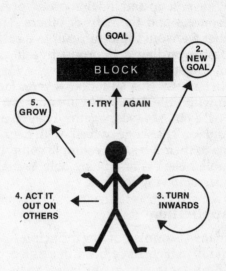

Figure 5.3. Responses to frustration

I. *Passive*. A person with little stress or challenge in their life and with low control can move into a passive state. This is seen in people who are chronically unemployed. With little to do we become passive or bored. Type-A individuals can find this particularly stressful and will move quickly into category II.

II. *Excessive stress*. If stress and demand in our lives increase dramatically but our control does not, we move into a state of distress. For example: having an important task to do and being frequently interrupted; not having the resources to do a job; attempting to juggle several tasks at once; being blocked and frustrated by bureaucracy.

III. *Active state*. When we have a large measure of control in a situation, we can respond more constructively to increased pressure or high work load. The stress becomes 'eu-stress' (see Figure 2.1) if we are able to make decisions affecting the outcome of our work, choose what we will do and in what order, or have full access to resources and the help of others. The same work load that we would find difficult in a category II state becomes rewarding and productive in category III, with a lot less stress.

IV. *Negative stress.* This situation is rare. However, some people with little demand in life may start to feel unfulfilled or even stressed again. They may need more demand or challenge which will help restore some balance to their lives. An example could be owning a profitable business and being able to make final decisions, but not having to work.

Practical Application

There are many examples of the principle of taking control, some of which have been discussed already. Stress from disorganisation in our lives can be reduced when we plan clearly and deal with our problems in an orderly fashion. Conflict and misunderstanding in relationships can often be eliminated or minimised when communication improves. Burnout can be reversed when we make lifestyle changes that restore our balance (see Figure 2.1.). Our stressors may not change, but we will. Worrying about something is a futile activity and only causes more distress. Jesus warned us about this.[38] A change of attitude towards the thing or person involved will reduce our distress, or even eliminate it. Handing over a burden to where it belongs replaces stress with peace.[39] Prayer always changes us, even if God does not change our circumstances.

This is a biblical principle. Paul wrote to the Philippian church in Asia Minor, while he was in a Roman prison, waiting for his execution. We would never have guessed his circumstances from the way he wrote. He was totally confident that God was in charge (Phil 1:6); unmoved by the prospect of imminent death (1:21); uncomplaining, and encouraging others to live that way (2:14); pressing on towards his goal. (3:12–14) He replaced anxiety with joy (4:4), and through prayer experienced peace of heart and mind. (4:6–7) The key was in being in control of *himself*, not his circumstances. *Self-control* is the summation of the fruit of the Spirit in our lives.[40] It is evidence of maturity in the Christian life.[41] We know from the Gospels that self-control was something Peter needed to learn. Clearly he did learn it, and later he wrote about this strength.[42]

RENEWING THE MIND

Our minds are not closed systems. They are constantly being influenced by new information and ideas. Some people find this threatening and resist any thought of change or growth. They cling doggedly to old ideas, not necessarily because they are convinced of their truth, but because they are afraid to bring them to the light and examine them. An important part of intellectual wholeness is a willingness to review our beliefs and behaviour in the light of new information. We can then make changes as a result of fresh insights if we need to, or else we can re-affirm our original belief. Regular flossing of the mind prevents truth decay.

If something is true, we have nothing to fear. Jesus said: 'You will know the truth, and *the truth will set you free.*'[43] This principle applies to all truth, not only to Christ's teaching. It may necessitate making changes in our physical lifestyle, emotional development or relationships, in the light of new information. The term *'renewing the mind'* comes from the New Testament. Christians are urged not to 'conform any longer to the pattern of this world, but be transformed by the renewing of your mind'.[44]

When our minds have been opened to God, we may still have a lot of work to do to change our worldly mind-set or frame of reference. Our minds (thoughts, attitudes, wills) need renewal because they have been secularised. Paul tells us that when people become Christians, their minds are open to the Spirit of God, so that they can now have 'the mind of Christ'.[45] However, this does not happen automatically. We have

		DEMAND	
		LOW	HIGH
C O N T R O L	LOW	I PASSIVE	II STRESS ++ (Distress)
	HIGH	IV NEGATIVE STRESS	III ACTIVE (Eu-stress)

Figure 5.4. The stress/control relationship

to desire it and consciously bring our old value system to the light, allowing God's Spirit to change our thinking. It involves a radical paradigm shift, and applies to every thought. Harry Blamires, in his book *The Christian Mind* says, 'There is nothing in our experience, however trivial, worldly, or even evil, which cannot be thought of Christianly.'[46]

Changing Your Mind

In Chapter One we described how our belief system ('mind') determines all our behaviour (see Figure 1.3.). The mind is the battleground where decisions are made which affect our behaviour. If this is so, how do we as Christians 'change our minds' so that we have 'the mind of Christ'? Paul gives us a model for doing this:

> The weapons we fight with are not the weapons of the world. On the contrary, they have divine power to demolish strongholds. We demolish arguments and every pretension that sets itself up against the knowledge of God, and we take captive every thought to make it obedient to Christ.[47]

There are three steps to renewing your mind, and developing 'the mind of Christ':

1) *Identify the error*. A stronghold is anything that controls us. In this context it refers to thoughts, 'arguments and pretensions' which are inconsistent with 'the knowledge of God'. In other words, erroneous beliefs, values or attitudes that we may have acquired from our family modelling or worldly culture. Identifying them is the hardest part. That is why we have been given 'divine power' and weapons that are 'not of this world'. These weapons are the Word of God, the Holy Spirit and spiritual discernment.[48]

2) *Take it captive*. Once I have identified my wrong thinking, I need to own it as mine, take responsibility for it and do something about it. This is how I 'take it captive'.

3) *Make it obedient to Christ*. This is the process of replacing error with truth and developing the 'mind of Christ'. In an attitude of prayer we rely on the Holy Spirit to 'guide us into all truth', as he promised.[49] We actively '*put off* your old self . . . to be made new in the attitude of your minds, and to *put on* the new self'.[50] This is something only *we* can do, in partnership with God.

133

SUMMARY

Intellectual wholeness requires that we develop health-promoting mental attitudes. It is important to keep a balance between left and right brain functions. Practical aspects of intellectual wholeness include learning to set effective goals, dealing with frustration when these are blocked, and increasing the amount of control we have in our lives. Our minds constantly need to be renewed and brought in line with the truth.

REFLECTIONS AND EXERCISES

1) Look through the left and right brain functions listed in Figure 5.1.

• Which ones are you developing, and are there some that you have neglected?
In what ways could you improve this balance?

2) ATTITUDES   With which of the eight mental attitudes that promote wholeness described in this chapter can you identify?

• Are there some that you would like to develop further in your life?
In what ways could you do this?

3) GOALS   Write out your specific life goals. Include as many as you can think of.

• Now arrange them in a *vertical order* of importance. Does this reflect what is actually happening in your life? What changes would you have to make to match up your goals with reality?
• Identify which of these goals are short-term, medium-term or long-term.
• Define one activity which would have the most significant, positive effect on your life, if you pursued it consistently.

4) Imagine that you wish to set up a small business, such as making toys or growing plants to sell in a market; or running an after-school childminding centre.

• Think through the goal-setting process using the what, why, where, how and when questions.

5) CONTROL   How much control do you have in your life, at home and at work? Can you relate the quantity of stress and pressure that you experience to areas where you have little control?

• In what ways could you increase the amount of control in your life, especially in areas where you are experiencing stress?

6) RENEWING THE MIND   Compare your values with those of Jesus, in the following topics. Think through and define your values first, then check the references to Christ's teaching on these topics (and any others you can think of) and compare them.

a) *Anxiety*   Matt 6:25–34; Mark 4:35–41
b) *Greatness*   Mark 10:35–45; Luke 9:46–48;
                        22:24–27
c) *Humility*   Matt 11:29; 23:11; John 13:3–17;
                        Phil 2:5–11
d) *Possessions*   Luke 12:32–34; 19:8–9
e) *Love*   John 13:1, 34, 35
f) *Forgiveness*   Matt 5:23,24; 6:12; 18:21–35
g) *Relationships*   Luke 6:27–42; 8:19–21
h) *Concern for*
   individuals   Luke 15:1–32; 19:1–9; John 8:1–11
i) *Authority*   Luke 4:31–37; 7:1–10; John 8:28, 29
j) *Attitude to life*   Luke 9:23–25; 14:26, 27

• Identify any areas where you may need to change your thinking so that you have 'the mind of Christ'.

## SIX

EMOTIONAL WHOLENESS

The full and free expression of all our feelings is necessary for personal peace and meaningful relationships.

John Powell[1]

Try to imagine a world without emotions or feelings – no love, no anger, no joy, no pain – just thoughts, logic and hard reality. On the other hand, picture a society where feelings are rampant, uncontrolled and dominating our lives. Both extremes are abhorrent, and clearly a balance in handling feelings is desirable. 'Much evidence testifies that people who are emotionally adept – who know and manage their own feelings well, and who read and deal effectively with other people's feelings – are at an advantage in any domain of life.'[2]

UNDERSTANDING OUR EMOTIONS

We were created with a unique set of emotions, similar yet different from those of other people. Our emotions and feelings are part of the core of who we are. We were not born with thoughts. These are derived from information and facts acquired from the world around us. We *own* our thoughts but we *are* our emotions. Knowing ourselves includes knowing our feelings, and yet for many people, their emotions are the least understood part of who they are. 'The surest sign of maturity is the ability to experience one's emotions freely and integrate them into all aspects of one's being.'[3] It is not possible to be a whole person if we are not growing in emotional wholeness.

Emotions and Feelings

Emotions

There are four basic emotions, which can be remembered by this mnemonic: GLAD, SAD, MAD, AFRAID. These four primary emotions each give rise to many feelings, illustrated in Figure 6.1.

These four basic emotions give rise to specific facial expressions that have been shown to be recognisable by cultures around the world, even isolated stone-age tribes in Papua New Guinea.[4]

Feelings

Most feelings can be defined as *an emotion plus a thought*.

For example:
satisfied	= 'glad'	+	contentment
compassion	= 'sad'	+	concern
lonely	= 'sad'	+	awareness of isolation
aggression	= 'mad'	+	beligerance
courage	= 'afraid'	+	determination.

There is considerable overlap between emotions and feelings, and the terms are often used interchangeably, but they are both distinct from our thoughts. Often people say things like: 'I feel that I need a walk.' This is actually expressing a thought, not a feeling. The person is really saying something like: 'I *feel* lethargic, or bored, so I *think* I will take a walk'. The statement, 'I feel that he should apologise' is clearly a thought made to sound like a feeling. Whenever the word *'that'* follows 'feel' (or is implied) a thought is being expressed, not a feeling.

Thoughts and Feelings

Which come first, thoughts or feelings? There are two pathways for our emotions. Sometimes there is a sudden, intense response, such as anger or fear, which precedes or is simultaneous with our thoughts. This is an involuntary reaction, mediated by the release of stress hormones and the body's autonomic nervous system. While we do not choose this reaction, it can still be modified or controlled by our thoughts.

There is a second type of emotional reaction which starts in our thoughts and results in a feeling, which is the more common pathway. Thoughts and attitudes usually precede and determine our feelings. The Cognitive Labelling of Emotions theory explains how this works.[5]

a) I experience an event, or have a thought
|
b) My body responds physiologically
|
c) I interpret this arousal and decide what emotion I am feeling
|
d) I experience this emotion.

Consider these examples:

• I meet someone that I have heard either bad or good things about. As a result:

a)I think negatively about that person/I think positively about him
b)My body tenses up when I meet him/I relax when I am with him
c)I interpret this as *dislike*/I interpret this as *pleasure*
d)I feel uncomfortable in his presence/I enjoy being with him

• a) I notice someone staring at me
  b) My heart beats faster.

  I can interpret this body response in a variety of ways, and the different interpretations will leadto different responses, e.g.:

(c)	(d)

It is nice that someone is interested in me   so I feel *pleasure*
I am unsure of the intentions of this stranger   so I am *afraid*   I
was hoping to remain anonymous   so I feel *frustrated*

- a) A banging noise wakes me up at night
b) I tense up and my heart races
c) I think it is an intruder trying   c) I remember there is a broken
     to break in   shutter in need of repair
d) I feel *afraid*, and start worrying   d) I feel *relaxed* and go to sleep

Thoughts usually lead to emotions and feelings, and our beliefs or attitudes are the frame of reference from which we choose our feelings. Our feelings often determine our actions. The word emotion is derived from the Latin '*motere*', which means 'to move', and the prefix '*e*' indicates 'away from'. Every emotion has the potential to lead to action. Thus it is vital to understand our emotions and feelings and to be *in charge of* them. This starts with self-awareness and the willingness to accept our feelings.

Accepting Our Feelings

Many people are confused about feelings because of cultural attitudes they have assimilated. The Stoics[6] had the erroneous belief that emotions are not good for us, and that mature adults should be able to repress their emotions with 'stoical fortitude'. Like so much else from ancient Greek culture, this attitude was absorbed into Western thinking.

I (John) was a nineteen-year-old medical student in England when I received news of my father's death in north-west China. I can clearly remember being belittled by my uncle because I cried. This reinforced for me the cultural stereotype that 'big boys don't cry'. The deeper message was: 'real men *don't feel*'. This seemed to be true, as I observed respected mentors and col-

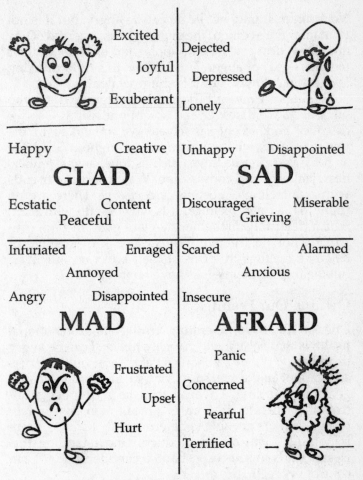

Excited	Dejected
Joyful	Depressed
Exuberant	Lonely
Happy Creative	Unhappy Disappointed
GLAD	**SAD**
Ecstatic Content	Discouraged Miserable
Peaceful	Grieving
Infuriated Enraged	Scared Alarmed
Annoyed	Anxious
Angry Disappointed	Insecure
MAD	**AFRAID**
	Panic
Frustrated	Concerned
Upset	Fearful
Hurt	Terrified

Figure 6.1. The four basic emotions

leagues going about their work amidst the tragedy and pathos of a busy hospital in the East End of London.

This 'taboo' on emotions for men applies to most feelings, such as tenderness, fear and confusion. The 'cool' look is in. Even expressions of happiness or excitement are suspect, except perhaps at a football match. It seems that the only feeling males are permitted is *anger*. It may not be nice to be angry, but it is not unmanly. For women, the stereotype is reversed. They are allowed to cry, be emotional, and express all their feelings – except anger. Fortunately, this rigid thinking is changing slowly, but it is still prevalent.

Feelings are *normal*. They are an integral part of who we are. As we discover and accept our feelings, so we discover and accept ourselves. We are made in the image of God, who is portrayed throughout Scripture as having strong feelings, such as love, anger, tenderness, jealousy and compassion. We must make friends with our feelings.[7] Feelings are *neutral*. There are no 'right' or 'wrong' feelings. It is what we do with them which determines whether they are good or bad, constructive or destructive. We can speak of positive or negative feelings in terms of their effect on our lives, but feelings of themselves have no moral value.

Owning Our Feelings

One of the most liberating truths about emotional health is that *nobody can give you a feeling*. I can be angry or unhappy about someone's behaviour, but that person cannot make me angry or sad. If someone could give me a feeling, I would then be a 'puppet', controlled by others, instead of an autonomous human being. If others are able to determine my feelings, there is nothing I can do about them. Understanding this clearly leads to self-respect and a confidence that I can control my feelings.

It follows from this that I am also not responsible for anyone else's feelings. A lot of people base their behaviour (what they say or do) on how they think others will feel or react. This cripples healthy relationships. Behaviour should be based on what is *right and loving*, not on how others might feel about it. It is a big help in our own marriage relationship to know that we are not responsible for each other's feelings, only for our own behaviour. We care about one another's feelings, listen to them, will not deliberately provoke them, but we do not take responsibility for them.

Owning feelings means to *identify* them and acknowledge them, at least to ourselves. It includes exploring them in our minds, attempting to find out what is behind them. Feelings follow thoughts. Some feelings can lead on to other feelings. For example, when people are angry it may be because they are grieving, confused or fearful. It has been well said that 'anger is the child of fear'.

If we have difficulty in admitting the original feeling, anger may surface to cover it up. When we worked in a hospital setting, we observed how relatives were sometimes very angry with medical staff when a loved one died. Anger masked the pain of their grief that they did not know how else to express. Learning to identify feelings clearly gives us a better chance of controlling them.

Controlling Feelings

Emotionally immature individuals are often controlled by their feelings. They do not know how to deal with them adequately, so they either *bury* them inside and are overwhelmed by them, or else they *dump* them onto others. Emotionally-whole people are fully aware of their feelings, and also in charge of them. Physiological research into the working of the brain helps us to understand this. The brain does not have pain fibres itself, although it records pain. Under local anaesthetic, tiny electrodes have been inserted into the brains of people who are fully conscious to determine the function of different parts of the brain.

The electrical impulse from an emotional response can be picked up this way via an electrode placed in the area of the brain where feelings are recorded. It was found that a feeling will dissipate after about fifteen seconds, even an intense emotion such as anger. (See Figure 6.2.) We can, however, decide to keep a feeling going for more than fifteen seconds by 'recycling' it.

We also have the ability to control a feeling if we want to, especially after the first few seconds, when the intensity of that feeling drops to a manageable level. So the physiological mechanism for managing feelings is in place, but we still need to learn how to control feelings, We must also have the desire to do so. It takes time to 'un-learn' old habits and develop new behaviours. Failure to control our feelings has a negative effect on our health.

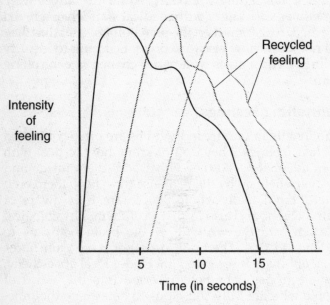

Figure 6.2. The duration of a feeling

Feelings and Physical Health

The effects of emotions on the health of the body has

been known for a long time. In the second century, the physician Galen[8] noted that depressed women were more prone to breast cancer than their cheerful counterparts. A thousand years earlier, Solomon said: 'A cheerful heart is good medicine.'[9] Modern research continues to establish a firm link between mind and body, emotions and health. The growing discipline of Psychoneuroimmunology (PNI) has discovered previously unknown connections between the mind, the neuroendocrine system and the immune system.

If feelings are not clearly identified and dealt with, they will be reflected in the body, a process known as the 'somatisation of emotions'. For example, a child who is fearful of going to school may develop stomach pains, which disappear after he is allowed to stay home, unless he has a physical illness. As adults, our stress and buried feelings are often expressed in physical symptoms too, such as headaches, diarrhoea, chest pains and many others. This phenomenon was described in Chapter Two. Sometimes an emotion, such as fear, can be incapacitating and even life-threatening.

I (John) will never forget a patient that I was responsible for as a resident doctor at Christchurch Hospital in 1955. He was a fit man, scheduled for a simple non-urgent operation for removal of the gall bladder. He told me that he was fearful because both his mother and an aunt had died following this particular procedure. I assured him that his surgeon was very competent, and that anaesthetic and surgical techniques had improved greatly in the intervening years. So he agreed to go ahead.

The operation was totally successful, but the following day his pulse rate increased and continued to rise alarmingly. He did not have an infection or other complication, but he died two days later. The post mortem examination revealed no evidence of bleeding or any problem with the operation site. A physical cause of death could not be established. It seems clear that he died from fear. I vowed never again to convince people to undergo medical or surgical procedures with which they did not fully agree. Later, when we were involved in medical work in Papua New Guinea, we came across a number of instances where patients died because of panic, or where fear appeared to be the main component of their condition.

Many recent clinical studies show a clear relationship between emotions and disease. The data from over 100 of them has been brought together in a significant study entitled *The Disease-Prone Personality*.[10] It revealed that people with chronic anxiety, unremitting stress, long periods of sadness and pessimism, continued cynicism and suspiciousness, were found to have twice the risk of disease. These illnesses included asthma, arthritis, headaches, peptic ulcer and heart attacks, among others. Much has been written recently about Mind–Body medicine. A clear summary of the findings to date on this subject is outlined in a well-researched book *Emotional Intelligence*, by Daniel Goleman.[11]

Feelings and Emotional Health

While it has been shown that the intensity of an emotion has virtually gone after about fifteen *seconds* (Fig 6.1), emotional memory can linger on for many *years*, especially if the emotion is deliberately perpetuated and reinforced. Our emotions and feelings never go away unless we fully deal with them. This applies to both 'positive' and 'negative' emotions. 'Positive' feelings that we have had, such as joy, peace, hope and contentment are good memories that will enhance health and wholeness if they are reinforced.

On the other hand, 'negative' emotions such as bitterness, resentment, melancholy, fear and grief will destroy our wholeness if they are recycled and not processed adequately. Most people are better at holding on to their negative emotions than reinforcing the positive ones. Buried negative feelings are *toxic* and destructive if they are allowed to continue. They not only lead to physical illness, but will block emotional growth. Young children find it particularly hard to deal with these emotions, and tend to bury them in the subconscious, which can result in emotional disturbance later as adults. We will look at ways of dealing with these feelings later in this chapter.

Feelings and Relationships

Feelings are the raw materials with which we build intimate relationships. It is usually inappropriate to reveal our feelings to casual acquaintances or business contacts. However, if we fail to relate at a feeling level with those we care about, these relationships will remain superficial. As John Powell put it: 'If I don't know your feelings, I don't know you, and if I don't know you, how can I love you?' It is possible to 'fall in love' with someone without knowing their feelings, but it is not possible to 'grow in love' together until each other's feelings are shared and known.[12]

We have already commented on the difficulty many men have in sharing their feelings, even in the safety of marriage. One woman described their problem this way: I've been married to Stan for twenty-five years, and I still don't know him. I know his likes and dislikes and some of what he thinks, but he never tells me how he feels. He used to do so when we were courting, but from the day we married, he became just like his father, cold and shut off. I knock on the door, and it is as if nobody is home.

We have also met some couples where the woman has greater difficulty in dealing with feelings than the man, but this is unusual. The Chinese encapsulate this dilemma in a proverb: *'Tóng chuáng, yì mèng'*, meaning: 'Same bed, different dreams.'

Our parental and family modelling is the most powerful influence on our ability to handle feelings properly. This becomes more obvious after marriage, where we tend to 'act married' in the way we observed our parents relating as we were growing up. Marriage does not give us the ability to deal with feelings, it merely shows up our deficiencies. On the other hand, in the commitment of a loving relationship we can help each other develop this skill.

There is some evidence to suggest that a few individuals have a deficiency in the emotional pathways in their brains, such that they are unable to identify and process feelings at all. Psychiatrists call this rare condition alexithymia. However, most people who have difficulty in handling feelings can learn how to do so, if they want to.

We now turn to look at this process in more depth.

DEVELOPING EMOTIONAL MATURITY

Nobody is born emotionally mature. Young children are uninhibited in expressing their emotions, but soon learn that this can be risky. They find themselves in trouble, because adults in their lives may not be as comfortable with feelings and are threatened by children's freedom. So children learn to hide feelings. They are also exposed to the gender stereotypes described earlier. Emotional maturity is a growth process. It starts with an awareness of our feelings, then learning how to process them, and how to deal with the feelings of others.

Learning the Language of Feelings

There are literally hundreds of feeling words or expressions available to us, but some people are 'feelings illiterate'. I (Agnes) lived with someone like that for a number of years. Our conversations about feelings would go something like this:

'How are you feeling, John?'
'Oh, fine, thanks.'

'But how are you really feeling?'

'OK.'

That seemed to be the limit of his feelings vocabulary . . . Yes, I (John) had difficulty identifying any feelings other than love or positiveness. I could not express, or even own 'negative' feelings such as anger, fear, disappointment or confusion. As we learned together how to express and receive feelings freely, it turned our relationship from black-and-white to technicolour.

Once people who are 'feelings illiterate' understand the need to develop in this area, it does not take long for them to discover this new world. They already have the feelings, and all they need to do is identify them and express them. This can be done by thinking about, and then talking about a whole range of feelings with someone who cares enough to listen. Using a list of feeling words can be helpful. (See Figure 6.3.) Think about each feeling, then write about it in your journal or talk about it with a friend. See also Exercises 1 and 2 at the end of this chapter.

# Anxious	# Frustrated	# Kindly	# Perplexed	# Virtuous
Arrogant	Fascinated	'Kinky'	Pessimistic	Victimised
# Brave	# Guilty	# Lonely	# Quiet	# Withdrawn
Bored	Grateful	Loving	'Queasy'	Worried
# Cautious	# Happy	# Misunderstood	# Relieved	# Youthful
Confident	Hopeless	Mischievous	Regretful	Yearning
# Disappointed	# Indignant	# Negative	# Sad	# 'Zany'
Defensive	Interested	Needy	Satisfied	
# Ecstatic	# Jealous	# Optimistic	# Thankful	
Envious	Jaded	Obstinate	Tender	

Figure 6.3 A sample list of feeling words.

Learning to Process Feelings

To process feelings is to identify them clearly and express them appropriately. Expressing feelings does not mean 'dumping' them on other people, or acting them out in an uncontrolled way such as a temper tantrum or sulking. Expressing feelings is the skill of haring them sensitively with another person.

Sharing feelings

Once I have identified a feeling and owned it as mine, I then need to express it in a clear 'I' statement, such as: 'I am sad', or 'I feel confused'. In these statements I am taking *ownership* of the feelings. To say 'You make me sad', or 'This confuses me', places the responsibility for my feeling somewhere else. It is a cop-out. Feelings are not opinions or objective facts but a subjective expression of what is going on inside. It is often appropriate to give reasons for our feelings, such as 'I am sad, because you forgot my birthday', or 'I am confused because I don't understand'. These are not blaming statements but provide more information.

There are two essential elements to healthy sharing of feelings: *honesty* and *love*. Without honesty, the exercise is phoney, but without love it can be hurtful. Paul states this principle in one sentence, in what is perhaps the greatest essay on relationships in all of literature:

> Speaking the TRUTH in LOVE,
> we will in all things *grow up* into him
> who is the Head, that is, Christ.[13]

This is a universal principle, not limited to growing in the knowledge of God. The emotional 'truth' at this time is my feeling, but I need to express it in a caring way. Two friends or partners who live by this maxim will be able to develop intimacy. Leave out either truth or love and the relationship falters. To express the truth honestly but hurtfully, or to withhold the truth in order to be kind, will destroy relationships.

Timing is also important in expressing feelings. The rule is to share feelings as soon as possible, particularly in important relationships, but sometimes it may not be appropriate to do so immediately. Others may be present who are not involved, something else may be more pressing, or the other person may be tired or upset. The feeling may be so intense that we need some 'time out' to gain control. However, the longer it is left before sharing feelings the harder it will be, and the more damage can be done to a relationship.

Another important rule is to share *one feeling*, or at the most two, at a time.[14] This will not burden the listener. If you have several feelings to share, it is helpful to check with the hearer to see if it is appropriate at this time.

Receiving feelings

For feelings to be useful in building relationships, both people need to be able to receive feelings. The art of receiving feelings is *just to listen* to them. When we were first married, I (John) could not do this. If Agnes told me about a feeling, I wanted to explain to her why she had it, especially if it was an uncomfortable one. Even worse, I might tell her why she ought not to have that feeling. At other times I would try to take the feeling away, to make her feel better. Sometimes she would say: 'I don't like being treated like a patient. All I want is for you to listen to me.'

Eventually I did learn how to really listen to her. Once Agnes was able to express her feeling fully to someone who was prepared to listen, the feeling often went away. It was also a great relief to me to know that I did not have to fulfil the male stereotype and provide an answer. I realised that my desire to find solutions to her feelings was really an attempt to make myself more comfortable.

FEELINGS CONTRACT

1) I will OWN my feelings

2) I will SHARE my feelings with you

3) I will not CLOBBER you with my feelings

4) I ask you to HELP me with my feelings

Figure 6.4. The Feelings Contract

A Feelings Contract

Eventually, we set up a feelings contract between us. We found this idea in David and Vera Mace's book *How to Have a Happy Marriage*,[15] and have adapted their contract slightly. (See Figure 6.4.) Our contract for dealing with feelings is in four parts.

1) *Owning my feelings*, as explained earlier, means identifying them and acknowledging them to myself. I accept responsibility for them and do not blame others for them. Owning them includes trying to understand them and also discovering what feelings may lie behind them.

2) *Sharing my feelings* means revealing them honestly and in a caring way to the person with whom I have this contract. I will not hide them from him or her.

3) *To clobber someone with my feelings* means using them destructively, for example: dumping my anger on the other person, sulking, being sarcastic or withdrawing emotionally. Some things which might seem like a 'clobber' to one person may not be obvious to another. So we need to be free within the contract to explain to

each other what we find hurtful, and promise not to use those behaviours to hurt or manipulate one another again.

4) *To help me with my feelings* means really listening to them and taking them seriously. I am not asking you to try to change them, but to know that you care and really want to understand what is going on inside me helps me to deal with them.

When this contract is applied conscientiously, it can revolutionise a destructive relationship. We have seen this happen with many couples. We encourage them to date it and sign it and put it up somewhere in the house where they can refer to it regularly. After a while, it can become a way of life, not only for a couple but for a whole family. This contract applies to handling all emotions, although one emotion requires particular care and attention: anger.

Handling the Tiger – Anger

Aristotle said: Anybody can become angry – that's easy! But to be angry with the right person, to the right degree, for the right purpose, and in the right way, that is not within everybody's power, and that is not easy.[16]

It is about 2,300 years since those words were written, but most of us can identify today with these same sentiments. As with all our emotions, anger is *normal* and healthy. We know from Scripture that God is at times angry. In fact, there are five times as many references to God's anger in the Bible as there are to man's anger. Because we are made in God's image, we too experience anger, and it is one of God's gifts. Anger is also *neutral*. There is no 'good' or 'bad' anger – just anger. What we do with it determines whether it becomes 'righteous' or 'unrighteous' anger.[17]

There are four basic ways people try to deal with their anger. (See Figure 6.5.)

a) Vent It

The commonest way is to explode or have a 'Vesuvius'. Our language is full of colourful idioms to describe this behaviour: 'blow your stack (or your top)'; 'spit tacks'; 'read the riot act'; 'get off your bike' and many more. Venting anger means *dumping* it on to someone, or *acting it out* in some way, such as yelling, physical aggression or having a temper tantrum. This may make the angry person feel better after 'letting off steam', but it does nothing to deal with the issue and is destructive of relationships. Venting anger does not dispel it, it actually feeds it, as shown in the diagram.[18] Being prone to anger has been shown to be a stronger predictor of premature death than smoking, hypertension or high cholesterol.[19]

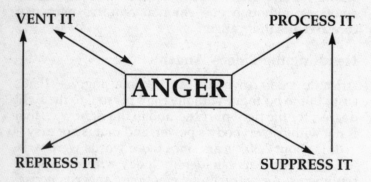

Figure 6.5. Ways of handling anger

b) Repress It

Anger can be banished to unconsciousness. This happens in children who have been hurt badly by a controlling or abusive adult. They may not even be aware of this buried anger, but it can surface years later in behaviour problems or depression. Repressed anger often emerges in other forms, such as emotional coldness, withdrawal from people, cynicism, sarcasm or bitterness.

Sometimes anger that has been repressed for years is vented, often in an explosion of violence, as illustrated by the arrow on the left in Figure 6.5.

c) Suppress It

By this we mean subduing one's anger *temporarily* until such time as it is appropriate to express it. This may be prudent. For example, anger at the boss could lead to dismissal. If the anger only concerns two people, others who may be present do not need to be involved. Hopefully, suppressed anger will be processed eventually (as the arrow on the right shows) otherwise it will be added to the pool of repressed anger.

In any situation anger needs to be controlled, which means suppressing it until we are able to handle it properly. The initial intensity of the anger is often too great, but after about ten seconds it is more manageable. (See Figure 6.2.) Some 'time out', however brief, is always needed to gain control over this powerful emotion. This is the main teaching of the Bible about anger management. It does not tell us not to be angry, but to be *'slow to anger'*. God is described as being slow to anger, and we are encouraged to follow his example.[20]

d) Process It

By this we mean using anger constructively, neither dumping it on others nor on ourselves. Anger must be acknowledged, owned and then expressed assertively but not aggressively. 'I feel angry because . . .' owns the anger as *my feeling* but leaves the other person free to dialogue with me. 'You make me angry . . .' is not a true statement, and will lead to a defensive response.

The closer the relationship between two people, the more important it is to tell one another when they are angry. The feelings contract will help, especially if it has been practised with less difficult feelings already. People who love each other can still be angry with one another. In fact, the more you love someone, the more that person could hurt you, even unintentionally. If anger is not processed between friends and lovers, it will result in coldness and lack of intimacy.

Using Anger Constructively

Anger releases *energy*. It is part of our survival kit to cope with challenge and danger, and this energy can be used constructively. We need more angry Christians, people who are angry enough about poverty, exploitation, hunger and injustice to do something about it. Unfortunately, many of us have been taught to think of anger as inherently bad, and to repress our anger. Paul wrote: 'Be angry, but do not sin',[21] not 'Don't sin by being angry'. The verb is in the imperative tense, so it is a command to use anger constructively and not destructively.

Anger turned out to be a big issue for Tony and Jan. In the last chapter we described the way Tony apologised for dumping his anger on Jan. He identified it as coming from frustrations in his job and nothing to do with her. As they developed their trust and communication skills, they were able to bring healing to past hurts.

Jan came to see in the counselling sessions that much of the negativity and frustration she experienced in their marriage had its roots in her buried anger. As a child, she had repressed her anger at being expected to take so much responsibility for the care of her disabled brother. She sublimated these feelings then by becoming a compliant, though reluctant, people-pleaser. She really loved Tony, but realised how she had placed unrealistic expectations on him to rescue her and meet all her needs. When this did not happen, she began to withdraw and they grew apart.

When Tony and Jan understood the reasons for their anger, they stopped blaming each other and making excuses. They apologised for hurts they had caused. This led them to forgive one another, which brought tremendous release and a renewal of their love. They incorporated the 'Feelings Contract' into their daily communication, for themselves and also with their three children. This enabled them to process all their feelings, not only their anger.

Feelings and Faith

The Christian faith is based on the solid foundation of truth and facts. Unfortunately, the place of feelings in relation to faith has been largely dismissed through the centuries. This is probably because most teaching in the Church is given by men, who often struggle in the feelings area. Many sermons are merely the transmission of facts from the head of the preacher to the heads of the listeners, without going through the hearts of either. This is an incomplete and distorted representation of God and the way he wants to relate to us.

God is a feeling Being. He is portrayed in Scripture as the God of love and compassion. One of the most beautiful Hebrew words used to convey this is 'chesed', which is translated loving-kindness, or love.[22] It is used 243 times in the Old Testament, frequently in the Psalms, and covers a range of meanings: love, mercy, pity, favour, compassion. It is mostly used of God, but sometimes of people, who have developed this quality too.[23]

Jesus came in human form to reveal to us what God is like.[24] As a man, Jesus expressed his feelings openly, and his biographers recorded the range of them.[25] In his interaction with people, Jesus was joyful as well as sad, angry as well as compassionate. His sense of humour comes through clearly in the Gospels in the form of humorous parables, irony and word plays.[26] 'Jesus never jests as Socrates did, but he often let a ripple of happy breeze play over the surface of his mighty deep.'[27] He also experienced tiredness, loneliness and depression. He became truly human, so that he could 'feel sympathy for our weaknesses.'[28] He provides us, men and women alike, with a model of a human being who was comfortable with, and able to express all his feelings.

To experience human intimacy, two people must be able to be real and share at a feeling level. Likewise, if we want intimacy with God we must relate to him at a feeling level too. God has revealed his heart to us, and he waits for us to be vulnerable and share our hearts with him. The psalmists were good at this: 'My soul thirsts for God'; 'my soul is downcast'; my heart is glad'; my heart has turned to wax'; 'I love the Lord'.[29] As we share ourselves with God in this way, so our relationship with him will grow.

SUMMARY

Emotional wholeness is an essential part of our maturity as human beings. Emotional development is lacking in many people who may have grown to maturity in the other areas of their person. To experience deep intimacy with people or with God, we must be in touch with our feelings, able to own them and express them freely.

REFLECTIONS AND EXERCISES

1) FEELINGS   Work though the list of feeling words (Fig 6.3) and reflect in your journal on these questions: When did you last have that feeling? How long did it last? What did you do about it? Were you able to share this feeling with anyone else, or with God? Do you still have that feeling?

• This is a helpful exercise to talk over with your husband/wife or a close friend.
  Use the 'feelings contract' in this process.

2)   Part of owning a feeling is to understand it and *describe* it. A helpful exercise is to take a number of feelings and explore what they mean for you, because each person experiences a feeling in a unique way. Here is how two people experience fear:

When I am AFRAID I feel uncertain,	When I am AFRAID I feel bewildered,
When uncertain I feel confused,	When bewildered I feel paralysed,
When confused I feel insecure,	When paralysed I feel lost,
When insecure I feel lonely,	When lost I feel abandoned,
When lonely I feel SAD,	When abandoned I feel REJECTED.

Notice that each has a different spectrum of feelings to describe their fear. One ended up sad and the other rejected.

- Try this process with a range of feeling words. Do it with a friend or your partner and discover how you each experience a feeling differently.

3) ANGER   Think about how you respond to anger and express it. Are you most often a 'represser', a 'venter' or a 'processor'? If you are aware of suppressing your anger frequently, is this so that you will be able to process it more effectively later, or does it usually end up being repressed?

Working this through with your friend or lover will help you grow in your relationship. People are often attracted to someone who deals with anger in a different way, and this can become frustrating unless they both understand what is happening.

4) Psalm 109 is a good model for handling anger. Read it through, preferably in a contemporary version such as The Living Bible. Notice four stages in the process:

a)Verses 1–5   David defines the problem
b)   6–20   He fully expresses his anger to God
c)   21–29 His attitudes changed after letting go
                 of his anger
d)   30,31 The result is his ability to praise God
                 freely.

5) If you are angry with a person who may have died, even a parent, or someone with whom you are no longer in contact, this can still be dealt with. Try this simple process:
a) Write down all that you are angry about or hold against that person. Take your time. Be as thorough as possible.
b) Imagine that person sitting in an empty chair opposite you, then read out loud what you have written to him or her.
c) If you are ready to do so, offer forgiveness to that

person. Ask God for forgiveness for your part in the whole story.

d) Hand over the letter to God. Symbolise this by burning it.

6) FEELINGS AND GOD   In your devotional time, start telling God your feelings: about him, about your life and circumstances and about yourself.

- You may find it easier to write them in your journal as a prayer.
- It could be helpful to read a Psalm first.

## SEVEN

SOCIAL WHOLENESS

No man is an island, entire of itself;
every man is a piece of the Continent, a part of the main.

John Donne[1]

We all start life as part of another human being: our mother. Child psychologists assure us that it is at least seven to nine months following birth before we become aware of ourselves as separate individuals and appreciate the 'independent and permanent existence of others'.[2] With that growing awareness comes a desire for social interaction, firstly with parents or care-givers and then with other people. Children are naturally curious about other children and reach out to one another, if given the opportunity. Human beings are gregarious and do not like to be isolated from others. This desire to socialise is a direct consequence of the fact that God has created us in his image to live in community, as he does: Father, Son and Holy Spirit. We were not designed to live in isolation.[3]

BELONGING

We all have a great need to feel that we *belong*. We can belong in many ways: to our family, culture, social group, peer group, professional or work setting or perhaps to a church. Without a sense of belonging, people feel rootless and insecure. This is one reason some young people join gangs to provide a sense of identity. The urban population drift and high mobility in

Western society, with the consequent loss of the extended family network and sense of group identity, is part of the cause of the social breakdown today.

One little boy grew up in a family who moved every two or three years because of his father's work. One day, he asked his mother, 'Where did I come from?' She saw this as an opportunity for some sex education, and so explained where babies came from. 'Oh dear,' he said, 'I thought I came from Sydney!'

We all have a deep need to discover our 'roots' and to identify our place in the world. Both of these are important for the development of a sense of identity and also for our growth to wholeness. John Powell writes:

> The inescapable law built into human nature is this: We are never less than individuals, but we are never merely individuals . . . Butterflies are free, but we need the heart of another as a home for our hearts. Fully alive people have the deep peace and contentment that can be experienced in such a home.[4]

THE COSTS OF SOCIAL ISOLATION

The damaging effect of loneliness and isolation to the *physical* health of human beings has been well established in many studies.[5] A combination of factors such as lack of human companionship, chronic loneliness, social isolation and the loss of a loved one predispose a person to premature death. Death rates for single, widowed and divorced people of all races and ages has been shown to be significantly higher than for married individuals, for virtually every cause of death.[6]

Social isolation also affects us *emotionally* and *spiritually*. People who have been on their own for a long time can become strange and find communication difficult. We have also been designed to relate to one another in spiritual community. People without a spiritual foundation to life attempt to fill this void in many ways. Some move into a life of frantic activism or endless superficial socialising, seeking fun and diversion. Many people fill their lives with busyness and become workaholics, trying to fill spiritual emptiness with activity. Other common substitutes are alcohol, food, drugs or promiscuity. All addictions are evidence of a missing or weak spiritual dimension to life. They represent a spiritual search.[7]

There is a big difference between social isolation and *chosen solitude*. We all need periods of aloneness just as much as we need to be with people. We can be alone without being lonely. 'Loneliness is inner emptiness; solitude is inner fulfilment.'[8] To be socially whole, we must build times of solitude into our lives, when we can stop, listen, relax and re-focus. Solitude and silence provide opportunities for us to find direction and vision, to listen to God and to others. From our solitude we can bring richness into our social lives. Dietrich Bonhoeffer wrote: 'Let he who cannot be alone beware of community. Let he who is not in community beware of being alone.[9] We explore further the value of solitude and silence in the next chapter.

SOCIAL DEVELOPMENT

During the first two years of life, a vital part of a child's social development is the emergence of *basic trust* and a feeling that the world is a safe place. Conversely, some children develop a mistrust of people and of their environment. Erik Erikson showed that the degree of trust/mistrust that we have greatly influences our social development.[10] As children continue to grow, increasing self-awareness enables them to develop some autonomy. This usually brings them into conflict with others, particularly their parents. Their favourite word tends to be 'No!', and they want to do more and more things for themselves. This is part of the socialising process.

We all start life totally self-centred, believing that the world revolves around 'me'. This is because for an infant it usually does. Everything is provided for babies, who are incapable of fending for themselves: food, comfort, protection, cleaning, warmth and sleep. Their needs are usually met in response to a cry or a smile. We begin life in a world-of-one, and it can be a hard lesson to discover that life includes others who also have needs, which may be as great or greater than our own.

The story is told of the Chinese sage who had a profound dream. In his dream he was having a conducted tour of the after-life. His guide took him first to hell, and he was surprised to see everyone seated at a banquet. The food was magnificent and the aroma wonderful, but the people looked starved. Each was equipped with a pair of chopsticks three feet long, and none of them was able to eat a mouthful. The guide then took him to visit heaven. The scene was the same. Everyone was seated at a sumptuous feast and also equipped with long chopsticks. However, these guests were really enjoying themselves, because each was feeding the person opposite.

Social wholeness requires that we move from being *self-centred to other-centred*. This is not done by negating ourselves, but through developing a sense of self-worth. Only then we can forget ourselves and focus on the needs of others. (In *Created for Love*, we explore more fully how to grow in healthy self-esteem.[11]) Other-centredness can become a way of life, loving your neighbour as yourself.

Many adults continue to live in their childhood 'world-of-one', still seeing themselves as the centre of their universe. They base decisions on how it will affect them personally, and relationships are evaluated in terms of 'What's in it for me?' This is sad, because people wrapped up in themselves make very small parcels. Self-centredness prevents the development of social wholeness, or even the desire for it.

Within each child is a healthy drive for *independence*, to explore and grow. Some children find the journey to independence harder than others, perhaps due to having a shy or timid personality. Other children are slowed down by a clinging parent who is reluctant to allow their child to leave his or her control. Parents sometimes use their children to meet their own emotional needs.

Social wholeness takes place in stages, and is a progression from:

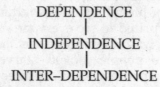

DEPENDENCE
|
INDEPENDENCE
|
INTER–DEPENDENCE

Inter-dependence is not the same thing as *co-dependence*. In a co-dependent relationship, one person is inadequate in some way and the other supports their 'pathology' by becoming a rescuer. Two people experience healthy inter-dependence when they both contribute constructively to each other's lives and value each other's company. They are both concerned about each other's welfare. They like to be with each other, but do not *need* each other to survive. They respect each other's 'boundaries', and can move comfortably between intimacy and autonomy in their relationship. This requires good communication skills.

Social Wholeness Through Good Relationships

Many books have been written on the subject of communication.[12] Here are four basic relationship attitudes that we require in order to relate well socially. They all are part of what it means to be other-centred.

a) Listening

By listening to you, and giving you my focused attention, I convey to you that you are important to me. Listening is loving. Many people have seldom been listened to, especially as children. Consequently, good listeners are rare. Not many of us have seen listening modelled by others or have experienced the pleasure of being listened to very often. Listening affirms us and builds a sense of worth. Listening heals. Besides, people often become more interesting when they stop talking. The ancient wisdom still holds true: 'Be slow to speak and quick to listen.'[13] Listening is a skill to learn, but it begins as an attitude.

Listening is *hard work*, especially for people who talk a lot. I have to deliberately turn the focus of attention from me to you, and set aside my own agenda in order to pay attention to yours. I must leave where I am and go to where you are, sit in your chair or walk in your shoes for a while. When I really listen, I am trying to understand who you are as well as what you are saying. The ancient story of Job illustrates the point. Job's comforters were the most helpful when they sat with him in silence for seven days. When they started to talk and offer advice, it became so bad that God told Job to pray for them.[14]

LISTEN!

When I ask you to listen to me, and you start
giving advice,
you haven't done what I asked.
When I ask you to listen to me, and you begin to
tell me what I
shouldn't feel, you're trampling on my
feelings.
When I ask you to listen to me, and you try to

solve my problems,
you have failed me, strange as it may seem.
Listen! All I ask is that you listen.
Not to talk, or do – just to hear me.
Advice is cheap. A few cents will get 'Dear Abby'
and
Billy Graham in the same newspaper.
I can do that for myself; I'm not helpless –
discouraged
and faltering, but not helpless.

When you do something for me that I can and
need to
do for myself, you contribute to my fear and
weakness.
But when you accept as simple fact what I feel,
however irrational it may seem to you, then I
stop
trying to convince you and can get on with
the business
of learning to understand what is behind my
feeling.
When that is clear, the answers are obvious,
and I won't need your advice.
So, please listen and just hear me.
And if you want to talk, wait a minute for
your turn,
and I'll listen to you.

Robert A. Hatcher

b) Respect

Close relationships are built on respect for each other's integrity and character. When respect goes there is not much left in a relationship. The word respect comes from the Latin, *respecare*, which means to look at. Looking people in the eye and communicating with them face to face shows respect. (It is appreciated that eye contact is not polite in some cultures, e.g. Maori

168

and Samoan.) However, looking at you means that I acknowledge you as a person and am not ignoring you. Respect is earned, but cannot be demanded. It is a gift which honours you for who you are.

c) Acceptance

To fully accept another person is a powerful gift of love. When people know that they are accepted they feel secure. You may not like some things that I do or say, but if I feel accepted by you *for who I am*, it helps me grow as a person. It gives me confidence to change things that others may find difficult in my behaviour. John Powell put it well: 'If those who love us will only accept us *in process*, that will be the greatest gift of their love to us.'[15]

d) Self-revelation

Being other-centred involves taking the risk of revealing who I am to you. This is scary, because you may not like what I show you. However, an important part of social development is being able to do this with at least one other person, and hopefully a few more. This presupposes that I *know* who I am, *like* who I am, and have developed the skills of sharing myself at a *feeling* level, as described in the last chapter.

Social Wholeness Through Growth

Mature, whole people are always growing. Knowing who we are is the foundation of social wholeness and healthy relationships. If I do not know who I am, I cannot be who I am in genuine encounter with others. Knowing myself starts with awareness of my strengths and limitations. This begins by understanding how my own body functions and then living in harmony with my body, seeing it as my best friend. It includes being comfortable with my sexuality. Failure at this level can lead to a lot of stress and breakdown in relationships.[16]

Understanding our own personality brings freedom and focus to living. This process takes time, but it is time well spent. A number of tools are available to help us in this search, such as the Myers-Briggs personality type tests and the Enneagram.[17] Awareness of, and being comfortable with our feelings is an important part of the process. Because we are spiritual beings, discovering our spiritual nature and knowing ourselves at that 'heart' level is another essential part of growth. I can only be socially whole when I relate to others as a whole person.

We must know ourselves before being able to reveal ourselves to others, but we cannot fully know ourselves in isolation. We need to interact socially with others in honesty and trust in order to grow. Part of a healthy friendship, especially in marriage, is helping one another to grow and become the person we were each created to be.

Social Wholeness Through Conflict

Many people believe that conflict and intimacy are mutually exclusive; that there must be something wrong with a relationship if conflict arises. In fact, the reverse is true; there is probably something phoney about a relationship where there is no conflict. Conflict is inevitable between two unique people, who have different personalities, background, values, interests or gender. Gender differences have been well described by a number of authors.[18] When two rivers meet there is always turbulence until they blend together downstream.

The real issue is not whether there is conflict in our relationship, but *how we deal with it*. We need to learn how to 'fight fair'. As we face the conflict between us we will understand each other better. By attacking the problem and not each other we have a good chance of resolving the conflict and growing in our relationship. To avoid conflict may ease the discomfort temporarily, but will lead either to an escalation of the problem, or else to a coldness and distance in our relationship.

People enter relationships with *different expectations* of what they want from them. If they do not share these expectations with each other, they are working on different agendas, and this will inevitably lead to misunderstanding and conflict. One person may want a closer relationship than the other. One may want to do most things together, whereas the other desires more freedom and autonomy. This is particularly true with regard to the degree of closeness or intimacy that a married couple expect to have with each other. The ultimate goal of intimacy is *to know and be known*; to be able to reveal myself to someone who really cares about me, and to receive that in return. When this is the expectation of marriage for one or both partners and it does not happen, a deep sense of loneliness can result.[19]

Many people desire this degree of intimacy yet fear it at the same time. If I do not like myself, or have a poor sense of self-worth, I will not risk sharing my inner self with anyone. A person who has been abused, emotionally, sexually or physically as a child usually finds it difficult to be really close to another human being as an adult. Young children have no defence against powerful adults, and can only survive by withdrawing into themselves. They learn to live within a castle with thick walls: 'No one is ever going to hurt me again.'

Working through relationship conflict, whatever the cause, is a good way to grow in emotional wholeness. This is true for two people in a friendship or marriage, but also for groups. Nothing spoils the fellowship of a church more than unresolved conflict. In a business or any other social group, efficiency and harmony follow the practice of dealing with conflict within the group as early as possible. Avoiding the conflict builds resentment and frustration.

This was something which Tony and Jan eventually

discovered. For years they avoided dealing with their conflicts. They certainly had arguments and fights, but the issues behind these were seldom resolved. This resulted in a build-up of resentment, which emerged in the form of snide remarks and sarcastic comments from Tony, nagging or coldness from Jan. They had sex together occasionally to meet their physical needs, but it was not a joyous expression of love and intimacy. Each tried to resolve the growing disillusionment in their marriage in different ways. Tony sought solace in his work, at the pub, or watching sport. Jan became overly involved in their children's lives, but as they grew older they needed her less. This left her feeling empty and frustrated.

When their communication improved, things started to change. They began to really listen to each other, and it felt safe. Jan shared with Tony some of the hurts and frustrations that she had brought with her into their marriage, as well as her unrealistic expectation that marriage would solve them. It was a healing experience for her when Tony just listened to her feelings, and did not dismiss them or try to 'fix' them.

Tony shared his fears with Jan: 'Life has passed me by. I've missed out on any prospect of promotion at work, and I'm too scared to make a career change. Over the past few years we've grown further apart, and it seemed like I was losing it with you too. I've always wanted a close relationship, but all I've managed to do is push you away. I'm frustrated with my behaviour, but feel powerless to do anything about it.'

This conversation led to many more. They decided to set aside some time every day to share their hearts with one another, and talk about 'real' things. Occasionally they slipped back into their old patterns, because habits die slowly. However, they agreed never to go to bed with unresolved conflicts, however long it took to deal with them. As time went by, there were fewer issues to deal with.

CULTURAL PERSPECTIVES ON SOCIAL WHOLENESS

The principles outlined already are universally true, but there is a great range of cultural attitudes affecting social behaviour that need to be considered. We are clearly writing from the perspective of our own Western culture. It is important to acknowledge that other cultures view social wholeness somewhat differently. Space only allows us to mention a few examples here.

Social relationships in the West start with the strong belief in *individualism* and personal rights. People see themselves as autonomous and separate from others. We have clear 'ego boundaries' in social interaction, even in the family – 'I', 'me', 'mine'. Social relationships are entered into by contract between autonomous individuals. Other traditions emphasise self-transcendence rather than self-assertion; harmony with nature rather than control of the natural order; integration into a social totality rather than autonomous social solidarity.[20]

Since the Renaissance, the Westerner defines the self by saying, 'I think, therefore I am' (*'Cogito ergo sum'*)[21] The African says, 'I participate and share my life with others, therefore I am.' The Oriental says, 'I belong, therefore I am.' From our personal observation in Papua New Guinea, it seems that the Melanesian says, 'I live in this village, therefore I am.' This would be true of most Pacific Island cultures, and probably many others who live in villages. The Maori says, 'I know where I come from, geographically and tribally, therefore I am.' Those who have lost this sense of identity are often lost socially as well, what socioligists call 'social anomie'.

Traditional cultural perspectives continue to be blurred as we move towards becoming 'a global village'. The population drift to cosmopolitan mega-cities

173

means the melding together of many cultures. However, there is a lot of miscommunication between people of various cultures, because of their different perspectives.[22] In every situation, social wholeness comes about from healthy inter-dependence and a sharing of lives together. Different cultures may arrive at this by different routes: in general, the process in the West is via independence and autonomy; in the East through conformity and solidarity with the group.[23]

So far, we have been addressing social wholeness in the individual, but individuals make up society. The social health status of individuals, their attitudes, values and behaviour will determine the social health of the society.

SOCIAL FACTORS AND HEALTH

Many studies in different countries have shown the powerful effect of social relationships on health. In general, people with low levels of social contact were twice as likely to die as persons higher on the scale. This association appears to apply more to males than females. These studies have established a clear link between the number, frequency and quality of social relationships and mortality.[24]

One study of about 7,000 randomly-selected adults in California, followed up over a nine-year period, looked at the link between four specific social relationships and mortality: marriage, contacts with close friends and relatives, church membership, and other social groups. In each instance, people with healthy social ties and relationships had lower mortality rates than people without them. The more intimate ties of marriage, family and close friendships were stronger predictors than were links with church or other groups.[25]

The stress of isolation and lack of social contact depresses the immune system in a similar way that disruptive social contact does, such as the prolonged stress of marital dysfunction, or caring for a relative with a chronic illness. The poorer the quality of the marital relationship, the greater the depression of the immune system. Clearly, interpersonal relationships have a significant influence on our psychological and physiological responses.[26] These studies confirm facts we all know intuitively but may not acknowledge.

SOCIAL WHOLENESS AND THE CHRISTIAN FAITH

The Bible is more about relationships than theology: how to relate to God and to people. It is filled with hundreds of case histories, focusing on how well the characters succeeded in these tasks. There are few success stories. We are emphatically told that you cannot claim a good relationship with God unless you love people:

> If anyone boasts, 'I love God', and goes right on hating his brother or sister, thinking nothing of it, he is a liar. If he won't love the person he can see, how can he love the God he can't see? The command we have from Christ is blunt: Loving God includes loving people. You've got to love both.[27]

The messages proclaimed by the Old Testament prophets were essentially about two things: total commitment to a heart relationship with God, and a concern for social justice.[28] This is the essence of the ten commandments: the first four are concerned with how we relate to God, and other six are about how to treat people.[29] The word *respect* summarises all the commandments. Relationships are also a major emphasis of the New Testament, and thirty per cent of the content of the Epistles deals with our relationships.

A right relationship with God must lead to right

relationships with others. True Christian faith starts in a person's heart, but it is proved real when demonstrated outwardly. Micah expresses the burden of all the prophets in the famous words: 'He has showed you, O man, what is good. And what does the LORD require of you? To act justly and to love mercy and to walk humbly with your God.'[30]

Moses summarised the laws concerning our social responsibilities in just five words: *Love your neighbour as yourself.*'[31] This command is repeated seven times in the New Testament by Jesus or his apostles[32] and Paul described it as a summary of the entire law.[33] When a pedantic legalist wanted to argue about 'Who is my neighbour?' Jesus told him the story of the 'Good Samaritan' which emphasises our responsibility to care even for our enemies.[34] He went so far as to say, 'Love your enemies and pray for those who persecute you.'[35] This principle is just as true today, and just as hard to follow.

Caring for my neighbour starts with those closest to me. 'If anyone does not provide for his relatives, and especially for his immediate family, he has denied the faith and is worse than an unbeliever.'[36] These are strong words. Many excuses have been given for avoiding this responsibility, but they do not carry weight with God.[37] A recurring theme in Scripture is God's concern for the poor, the fatherless, widows, strangers and the marginalised, and that this must be our concern too.[38]

What is God like? He is described as 'mighty and awesome' . . . yet one who 'defends the cause of the fatherless and the widow'.[39] When Jesus came to show us more clearly what God is like, he deliberately ministered to the poor, the sick, prisoners, the oppressed and outcast.[40] The Gospel records confirm that he spent the bulk of his time with such people. One of the most challenging statements of Jesus is that, in the ultimate analysis, the ones who will enter his kingdom are those who have demonstrated their faith by caring for the sick and prisoners, the hungry and thirsty, the strangers and the needy.[41]

SOCIAL WHOLENESS IN THE CHURCH

For all its failings, the Church is a spiritual community, the means that Christ chose to enable each member of 'his body' to grow. Many people today are frustrated with organised Christianity because they have not found a satisfactory fellowship. Some churches fail to adjust their approach or forms of worship to meet contemporary needs, or to present the unchanging Good News in relevant ways to a changing world. It is important to realise that we will never find the perfect church, and no church fellowship will suit everybody. The essential requirement is to be part of a church that adequately addresses our spiritual needs. We cut ourselves off from the Church to our own detriment.[42]

When Jesus completed his great work of salvation for the world and returned to heaven, he left his followers to be his agents and witnesses. Paul defines the Church as Christ's body, of which Christ is the Head and we are the parts.[43] We are his feet to reach the lost, his hands to heal the hurting, his eyes to see the needs of people, his heart to love a broken world. For a body to work effectively, it must function as a whole, with cooperation not competition, in harmony not discord. Each part is important and needs all the other parts. Paul explains that it would be ridiculous for the eye to say to the hand, or the head to say to the feet, 'I don't need you'. This metaphor of the body has two main applications:

Firstly, it implies that the members of the body will *care for one another* and become part of one another's lives. 'If one part suffers, every part suffers with it; if one part is honoured, every part rejoices with it.'[44] 'When you have a thorn in your foot, your whole body must bend over to remove it' (African proverb). Just as when one part of our human anatomy is injured, the rest of the body compensates and takes care of it until it heals, so we should be equally concerned and involved when one member of the Church is wounded or hurting. Often this is not so, and when one member fails or sins, others are quick to judge and criticise. The Church has been described as the only army which shoots its own wounded.

Practical aspects of 'body life' are spelled out in many ways in Scripture, such as: acceptance, kindness, forgiveness, patience, encouragement and sharing each other's burdens.[45] These all imply action and a reaching out to others. They result from right attitudes within, are motivated by love, and if put into practice will bring wholeness to the body. The sad truth is that perhaps eighty per cent of problems and failures in church life, in Christian organisations, and on the mission field are due to the breakdown of relationships. A historical example of this is the clash in the first missionary team between Paul and Barnabas, though there is evidence that this was healed.[46]

The other clear application of this metaphor is that the parts of a body are designed to work together. Jesus had a great desire that 'his body' would work in true harmony and unity. We know this from the wonderful prayer that he prayed to his Father, just a few hours before he was arrested and led away to die.

I pray . . . for those you have given me . . . so that they may be one as we are one . . . that all of them *may be one* . . . May they be brought to complete *unity* to let the world know that you sent me and have loved them even as you have loved me.[47]

Do we share this burden too? Brian Hathaway comments: 'We flock to seminars on evangelism, church growth, worship, signs and wonders and counselling, but what about seminars on unity? Seminars on unity aren't offered. Nobody would attend.'[48]

FELLOWSHIP AND COMMUNITY

True fellowship (*koinonia*) in the Church can only happen when the members of 'the body' are in right relationship with one another and also with their 'Head'. As in the human body, the individual parts cannot function unless they are connected to and controlled by the head. The Holy Spirit can turn the organisation of the Church into a living organism. Fellowship does not just happen, it has to be desired and worked for by each member of the body. In a large congregation it can be hard to feel a sense of closeness and fellowship. Here are some practical ways that social wholeness can be developed in a church.

Small Groups or 'Cells'

These can take different forms, perhaps two or three people meeting together regularly to share their lives and struggles, study the Scriptures and to pray for one another. For many years we have been part of a number of different kinds of small group designed for emotional and spiritual growth, usually with about eight to ten people. These provide wonderful opportunities to share with others at a deep level, and encourage the development of social wholeness as well as individual maturity. Elsewhere we have described the value of small groups in developing friendships and intimacy;[49] and also how to run growth groups.[50]

One movement, which is growing in popularity, is the Renovaré Spiritual Formation Groups, promoted by Richard Foster. Their emphasis is on developing a *balanced* spiritual life, drawing from the five main Christian streams: the holiness, charismatic, contemplative, evangelical and social justice traditions.[51]

Church Home Groups

The Church started as a small group movement, mostly meeting in one another's homes. Jesus modelled this by devoting the bulk of his time to a group of twelve people, and an inner core of three. The early Christians met in homes for most of their activities, such as instruction, communion, prayer and evangelism.[52] The churches in Corinth, Rome and Ephesus would have been associations of such small groups scattered throughout the city. Because of persecution, house churches remained the norm until the third century, when church buildings and cathedrals began to replace them.

The value of Christians meeting in small groups was rediscovered in the eighteenth century in the Wesley revival in Britain. Smaller groups called 'bands', averaging six people, and 'Class Meetings' with about ten to twelve people sprang up. These met weekly for support, fellowship, and on-going pastoral care of new Christians. Over the past thirty years or so, there has been a resurgence of the home as the meeting place for Christians, either as small independent churches or as cells that are part of a larger church fellowship.[53] In China, the rapid growth of the Church, with an estimated 20,000 new believers a day, has been made possible through a vast network of unofficial house churches. In the West, the churches which are growing fastest are those who place an emphasis on home groups.

Meeting for worship and instruction in small groups, whether in homes, factories, offices, schools, universities or restaurants, provides opportunity to foster social as well as spiritual wholeness. It provides opportunity to minister to one another in a way which is difficult or impossible in a large congregation. 'Let us not give up meeting together, as some are in the habit of doing, but let us encourage one another – and all the more as you see the Day approaching.'[54] The Greek word translated 'to encourage' is *parakaleo*, which means to come alongside to comfort, encourage and exhort. This is the way we grow ourselves and help others to grow in social and spiritual wholeness.

Christian Communities

There has been a growing trend worldwide towards the formation of Christian communities of various kinds. Community living is also popular in a secular context, for support, protection or to promote an alternative lifestyle. Two essential qualities for successful community are a sense of significance and a feeling of solidarity.[55]

Some communities are organised as an informal cluster of houses. Co-housing communities have been popularised in Denmark and other Scandinavian countries over the past two decades, both to increase a sense of community and for economic reasons. They share resources, meals, childcare and land for gardening or playing areas.[56] Sometimes two or more families decide to share a large house together.

After our own children left home and married, one by one they decided to return and live together with us for periods of time, from months to years. We set some new groundrules. They were not just coming back 'to live with mum and dad', but we shared costs, responsibilities and decision-making in the community. This provided a wonderful opportunity to develop friendships with our children and their partners as independent adults and equals. A community that includes three generations combines memories of the past, vision for the future and an opportunity to fully explore the present. Two of our daughters and their husbands spent some years leading a Christian community.

Friends of ours, Geoff and Gail Stevens, have lived in a variety of communities for thirty-five years. They are conscious of the danger of communities becoming in-grown and the need to integrate with the wider community to survive. Just as individuals must become other-centred to be socially healthy, so a community must have a common purpose that cares for others. There are many examples of Christian communities that have done this well, such as the L'Arche communities for the mentally handicapped; Mother Theresa's communities for the poor and the dying; L'Abri and Taizé communities helping young people on their spiritual quest; communities for helping drug addicts, street kids and AIDS victims.

A community is an ideal place in which to grow to social wholeness, moving from egoism to love, or as Jean Vanier puts it, 'making the transition from the community for myself, to myself for the community'.[57] A Christian community provides a place to grow, share your gifts, learn the meaning of acceptance and forgiveness, discover how to become a servant and live out Kingdom values.[58] Some traditions of the Church have emphasised the importance of Christian community, while others give more prominence to the individualistic expression of faith. As in all things, a balance is needed.

SUMMARY

Social wholeness is a benchmark of health. From the time of conception we are on the journey towards social maturity. It is not an easy ride, and demands conscious thought and effort. Different cultures may arrive by different routes, but to be socially whole is to be fully human. One of the major concerns of the Bible and of true Christianity is relationships, with consequent social responsibilities. Jesus prayed that his 'body', the Church, would be socially whole.

REFLECTIONS AND EXERCISES

1) Reflect in your journal about your own level of social wholeness. Maybe discuss it with someone who knows you well. How effective are your communication skills? Would you describe yourself as basically self-centred or other-centred?

- Write a description of the kind of person you would like to be in terms of social wholeness.

2) Imagine that you are attending your own funeral, and that someone who knows you well is giving the eulogy. What would he or she say about you in terms of your social life and how you related to others? Would you be missed from your community?

- What might you say about yourself?

3) Where do you belong? Make a list of places or social groups to which you feel a strong sense of belonging. Then discuss this in your small groups or with a friend.

4) Who is your neighbour? Is there any one from your family, friends or community that you have been neglecting? Think specifically about each member of your family or social network.

5) Who are 'the poor' for you? They could be financially poor people in your community or overseas. They might be poor in terms of friendship, encouragement or spiritual resources. Work through this in your journal or small group.

6) How much concern do you have for unity and wholeness in your church fellowship and for the Church at large? Are there any ways that you could help to improve oneness and unity in either situation?

- Brainstorm in your small group about possibilities. Then expand on these ideas prayerfully.

EIGHT

SPIRITUAL WHOLENESS

*There is a God-shaped space inside all of us
which nothing else can fill.*

Blaise Pascal[1]

A young man sought out a solitary holy man, eager to talk to him about prayer. The old man said nothing, but built up his small fire and made tea. He then began to pour the tea into the young man's cup. Though it was full, he went on pouring. The tea spilled all over the ground. The young man finally protested:

'It's already too full!'

'So it is with you,' said the old man. 'Until you are empty, how can you receive what you seek?'[2]

We cannot become whole persons if we fail to develop the spiritual dimension of our lives, we have to make space for this. As Augustine prayed, 'You, O God, have made us for yourself and our hearts are restless until they rest in you.'[3] In one sense all of life can be viewed as sacred, yet in another sense our spiritual nature is over and above the rest. Our spirits are eternal, the part of us all which will never die. Yet it seems ironic that for so many people this is the part which is the most neglected. After eleven years of imprisonment in Russian gulags, Solzhenitsyn[4] wrote, 'The object of life is not prosperity but maturity of the soul.'

A candle illustrates the three basic aspects of our make-up. The wax represents our bodies, the wick our minds and emotions, and the flame our souls. A candle functions best when it stands vertically. If you turn it on its side, the flame will splutter, the wax will melt and be wasted. Turn it upside down, with the 'body' on top, and the flame will be extinguished, leaving only a smell.

SPIRITUAL WHOLENESS

Spiritual wholeness results from being connected to God and growing in relationship with him. We have all been created with a spirit which has the potential for growth, but not on its own. Just as the candle needs to be lit from an outside source to become a light, so our spirits need to be brought alive by God's transcendent touch. This process is a profound mystery, but millions of people have found it a reality, and one day we will understand. 'We don't yet see things clearly. We're squinting in a fog, peering through a mist. But it won't be long before the weather clears and the sun shines bright! We'll see it all then, see it all as clearly as God sees us, knowing him directly just as he knows us!'[5]

Our finite minds can only understand a little of this mystery now, but God has revealed himself in creation, then in his word, and finally in Jesus Christ.[6] As we examine the life and teachings of Jesus we begin to understand a little about God. Jesus described himself as the way to God.[7] In discovering Jesus, we discover God as Father/Mother,[8] lover, protector, guide, friend and source of life. For some, this discovery has been a dramatic experience and a total revolution in their lives. For both of us it was more like the unfolding of a flower, an unconscious knowing as we were exposed to the truth, culminating in a conscious on-going commitment. For others it resembles the forward and backward motion of the waves as the full tide comes in.

Jesus spoke of loving God with heart, mind, soul and strength, and your neighbour as yourself.[9] Spiritual wholeness clearly includes the totality of who we are in our response to God. We cannot pinpoint what is happening in our spirits, but it is reflected in the other areas of our lives. The heart responds emotionally, the mind through understanding and application of the will, the body in how we behave, especially towards others. These function as a whole. We have explored these aspects of wholeness in previous chapters, and they all contribute to our spiritual wholeness.

Spiritual growth happens in conjunction with the development of the other areas of who we are. 'We cannot love and serve God with all our heart, mind, soul and strength if we have not yet found a mind and heart of our own.'[10] Jesus set the model for us, growing 'in wisdom and stature, and in favour with God and men.'[11]

The Holy Spirit

When Jesus had completed his task on earth and returned to heaven, he sent his Holy Spirit to carry on the work of producing spiritual wholeness in the lives of his followers by helping them to become like himself.[12] They must have found it hard to adjust from the physical to the spiritual companionship of Jesus, yet this was the best way for spiritual growth to take place in their lives as in ours. Many examples are given in the book of Acts showing the transforming power of the Holy Spirit indwelling those who followed the Jesus way.[13] The life lit by the flame of the Holy Spirit can then grow in spiritual awareness. This can be seen today, as it was in the days of the apostles, with fear turning to courage, weakness becoming strength and love growing in the lives of those who follow Jesus.

The Word of God

God has not left us to discover him by our own efforts or understanding, but has revealed himself in his word, the Bible. Jesus is identified as the Word.[14] This means that he is the expression of God, God in action, the way God has chosen to communicate himself to us. In the New Testament, two Greek words are used to describe this communication. The first is *logos* which is used 330 times, and refers to the written word of God, the Good News. The other is *rhema* which refers to the spoken word of God (usually as it is addressed to individuals) and is used 70 times. When we read the *logos*, we must seek the *rhema* or specific application to us now. In this way we come to know God personally, as the Holy Spirit opens our minds.[15]

There is always the danger of knowing about God but not really knowing him. As Jeremiah put it, 'You are always on their lips but far from their hearts'.[16] Jesus had the same problem in his day: 'You diligently study the Scriptures because you think that by them you possess eternal life. These are the Scriptures that testify about me, yet you refuse to come to me to have life.'[17] We must constantly be aware of the trap of studying the word of God, yet failing to discover the God of the word.

FALSE TRAILS

In our time in Papua New Guinea, we did a lot of trekking along jungle trails in order to bring medical help and the gospel message to people living in isolated places. Usually we were accompanied by a local guide. On one occasion we were visiting a village three days' walk from our hospital, in a remote area near the Sepik river. At one point I (John) offered to lead the way. It wasn't long before we came to a fork in the track and I chose what appeared to be the more obvious route, but it was actually a false trail used by wild pigs. This produced much laughter among our companions, and I stopped trying to lead the expedition.

So it is in our spiritual journey. There are many false trails which can divert us from the right path. Some of them seem good in themselves, with the promise of leading to the right destination, but turn out to be false trails. Here are a few of them.

Busyness

Excessive activity and work can be a cover-up for inner needs, such as unfinished grief, unhappy relationships or a deep dissatisfaction with life. A person with a poor self-esteem may become a workaholic in an attempt to prove their worth.[18] Workaholism is based on the belief that our worth is dependent on what we do, not on who we are. It can become an addiction which is just as real as an addiction to food or alcohol. It has been said that in our society people 'tend to worship their work, work at their play and play at their worship'.[19]

Workaholism has been described as a 'special addiction of the religious person' and can become a 'false religion'.[20] People who have been workaholics before becoming Christians have a tendency to 'baptise' their compulsion and see it as evidence of spirituality. Busyness, even in what we see as 'God's work' can keep us from an intimate relationship with Christ. Hard work is good but to fill every waking moment with work in order to prove something to ourselves, to others or God runs counter to the development of spiritual wholeness.

Materialism

Nothing dulls the appetite for spiritual wealth faster than material wealth. God has created a beautiful world for us to enjoy and loves to bless us materially, and in every other way.[21] However, Jesus warned us about the handicap that riches can be to entering the kingdom of God.[22] The 'prosperity gospel', which has been popular in certain quarters in rich countries of the West since the 1950s, does not match up with true Christian discipleship.[23] It is not that possessing wealth or money is inherently wrong. The issue is, do I own it or does it own me? Jesus summed it up: 'Where your treasure is, there your heart will be also . . . You cannot serve both God and money.'[24]

New Age Thinking

The essence of New Age philosophy is that we have all the answers within us for our health and spiritual wellbeing. One writer put it this way: 'As you grow spiritually, you are on a wonderful journey of self-discovery. Spiritual growth means growing through connecting with your Higher Self and a Higher Power – the God/Goddess within and without: Christ, Allah, Buddha, the All-That-Is.'[25] This is a *false trail*. It is like trying to lift yourself off the ground by pulling on your own shoe strings. It is true that many people have untapped inner strengths they need to release, and that they could grow immensely by discovering and developing their gifts. We touched on some of this in earlier chapters.

The journey of self-discovery also reveals to me my inadequacies and spiritual poverty. As I discover these, I am aware of my need to draw on God's strength and power to transform my life and enable me to grow in spiritual wholeness. The essence of New Age thinking is: 'I am the answer to all my own needs.' The essence of Christianity is: 'Only God, through Christ, can meet my deepest needs.'

Compartmentalising

By this we mean trying to separate the spiritual from the secular activities in our lives, having a Sunday religion which is not part of the rest of the week. Spiritual wholeness includes every aspect of life. A Christian doctor is not a doctor who happens to be a Christian, but a Christian who happens to be a doctor. Our spiritual value system must embrace and affect everything that we do, to be fully 'in the world but not of it'. Compartmentalised Christians are often 'of the world, but not in it'. Theologically they espouse the Christian belief system, but many of their attitudes and values are still controlled by unchallenged worldly thinking. Their minds are not fully 'renewed', as described in Chapter Five.

Limiting God

As we develop spiritual wholeness, so we grow in our view of God. The reverse may also be true. J.B. Phillips described in *Your God Is Too Small*, some of the inadequate pictures of God that people have, which may not have changed since their childhood.[26] Typical distortions are to think of God as:

- a policeman, constantly trying to catch me out
- a Divine rescuer, to be called on in emergencies
- a 'sugar-daddy', always there to pamper me
- a benign but out-dated grandfather, not on E-mail yet
- the Managing Director of the universe, too busy to care about me.

Being stuck with such pictures of God keeps us on a false trail. As we develop spiritual maturity, so our understanding and concept of God grows, even though he can never be fully known.

This is where Tony and Jan realised that they had gone wrong. In previous chapters we have described their growth in other areas. Although they had built some good things into their lives, the spiritual dimension was neglected. They had had a form of 'Sunday Christianity' which did not impact the rest of life. Now they became more open to discovering what God wanted for them, and saw the Bible as his word to them personally. Prayer became more meaningful. They were starting afresh on their journey into God together.

Spiritual wholeness does not just happen, it follows a deep desire for it and a willingness to become a *disciple* of Jesus. The word 'disciple' occurs 269 times in the New Testament. 'Christian' is only found three times, in reference to disciples.[27] The Church today has many Christian converts but few disciples, those whose goal in life is to become like Christ. Not long before Dietrich Bonhoeffer was executed in a Nazi prison, he wrote his challenging book, *The Cost of Discipleship*.[28] It is a blistering attack on 'easy Christianity' or 'cheap grace', as he calls it.

In the next section we describe some of the disciplines which are helpful in developing spiritual wholeness. It is only possible to refer to a few of these briefly in this limited space. Over the centuries, thousands of Christians have written far more eloquently than we can about ways to know God. We will share some ways that are particularly meaningful to us in our own spiritual journey.

PATHWAYS TO SPIRITUAL WHOLENESS

There are a number of disciplines that assist growth in spiritual wholeness. Some of these are indispensable to all who want to know God, and others will appeal to different personalities. We are all different, and God does not expect us to follow any set pattern in relating to him. We need to explore ways that others have found helpful, and discover what is right for us.

Prayer

'All of life is intended to be prayer. The purpose of human existence is to live in awareness of our creatureliness as this relates to a Creator, because this is our reality.'[29]

Prayer is *asking*. It is recognising that I have a need which could be met by another. So I pray with a sense of powerlessness. Jesus often taught about prayer and his life was full of prayer. There was nothing that he did without talking to God about it first.[30] This is a powerful model for us. Jesus said: 'Ask in my name, according to my will, and [the Father] will most certainly give it to you.'[31] Yet God does not want us to pray merely so that we will be dependent on him, but to build a relationship with him.

Prayer is *fellowship*, God and I communing. It is a mind-blowing concept to know that Almighty God wants to have a personal *relationship* with his creatures, but it is true. This means that I should not do all the talking, as prayer is intended to be a two-way conversation, not a monologue. Yet how little of our prayer, in private or in church, is listening to what God might want to say to us. If we spent as much time in listening as we do in speaking, our prayers would be very different. A human relationship would not last long if one person did all the speaking, and yet this is how we often treat God. Jesus spent many hours alone with his Father in prayer, enjoying his company, listening as well as talking. As we listen to God, he speaks into our spirits, telling us of his love for us, revealing his direction for our lives, and guiding us to wholeness.

Prayer is *individual* and unique to the person praying. 'Pray as you can, not as you can't.'[32] As each human relationship is unique, so my relationship with God in prayer is unique. This time spent with God is spiritual wholeness-building time, when my spirit becomes one with the Spirit of God. Closeness with God can be experienced all through the day, but we also need to set aside specific times for building this relationship, just as we would in a human friendship. As an engine needs to refuel in order to keep going, so our spiritual 'tanks' must be topped-up to maintain spiritual wholeness.

Prayer is *costly*. It takes time, effort, concentration and a willingness to make it a priority. This is not easy. Just as two lovers surrender to each other, so in prayer I surrender myself to the Heavenly Lover, to God who is love. 'True love is a giving of self to God, an opening of the self to God, not a seeking to feel God.'[33] We meet God on his terms, not ours. The purpose of prayer is not to make us feel good, although after time spent in prayer our spirits are often refreshed, calmed, renewed and in a real sense made whole.

Prayer is *receiving*. This seems a contradiction but is the result of 'asking prayer'. What we receive may not be what we expected, but is often far more.[34] The God we pray to is rich in mercy, abounding in love, full of compassion and longs for our fellowship. The wealth he wants to give us is only limited by our capacity to receive.

Prayer is *worship*. Prayer is one important way of leading us into the active worship of God. Evelyn Underhill defines prayer as that part of our conscious life which is deliberately oriented towards, and exclusively responds to God. She points out that while prayer begins as an intention of the intellect, it needs our feelings if we are to move towards God. Finally, it requires the determined fixing of our wills on God.[35]

In fact, prayer and worship are activities which

include our whole person. Prayer involves our *bodies*. The Hebrew words translated 'worship' means to bow down or prostrate the body. 'Bless the Lord' means to kneel. 'Thanksgiving' means to stretch out the hand. Paul tells us to 'present your bodies' to God as 'your spiritual act of worship'.[36]

Prayer must include our *minds*, even though thinking and reasoning may be lost as the Spirit leads us into worship. Paul said, 'I will pray with my spirit, but I will also pray with my mind.'[37] Prayer also includes our *emotions*. The Psalms are prayers that are full of emotions: 'My soul thirsts for God . . . my heart is glad . . . why are you downcast, O my soul . . . I love the LORD . . .' Forty-one of the Psalms command us to sing to the Lord as an expression of our soul's worship.

Prayer and worship are *social* activities as well as private. 'Glorify the LORD with me: let us exalt his name together.' 'Come, let us bow down in worship, let us kneel before the LORD our Maker.'[38] Ultimately, prayer is a *spiritual* activity, where our spirits meet with God's Spirit. 'God is spirit, and his worshippers must worship in spirit and in truth.'[39]

WAYS OF PRAYER

'Teach us to pray' was a request the first disciples made to Jesus, and all serious followers of Jesus since that time have desired this too. Jesus gave a short and concise model prayer, which includes all aspects of prayer that are needed in our part of the two-way process.[40] The *Lord's Prayer* helps us define the kinds of things we need to say to God. The other half of prayer is our listening to what God wants to say to us. 'The art of listening is at the heart of genuine prayer.'[41] Unfortunately, our spiritual ears are not always tuned in to the right channel. Sometimes we do not want to hear what he is saying to us. At other times we are too full of our own ideas.

It certainly stirs our hearts when we know God is speaking to us. Elijah heard him when he stopped long enough to listen to a 'gentle whisper'. Jeremiah records God as saying, 'I spoke to you again and again but you did not listen.' Joseph was warned by God in a dream to escape to Egypt with Mary and the Child. Paul not only heard a voice but was struck down by a bright light when Jesus spoke to him from heaven.[42] Like those people of Bible times, we too need to train our ears, minds and hearts to listen to the different ways God speaks.

There is so much we can learn about prayer from those who have lived before us. I (Agnes) learned to pray by hearing my mother pray and following her words. In the same way, Jesus' disciples overheard him talking to his Father and some of these prayers are recorded for us. John's Gospel chapter seventeen is an unique example of this. Down through the centuries some people have given their lives to prayer. The Desert Fathers and Mothers practised solitude and silence in prayer, something Jesus emphasised to his disciples.[43] Here are four traditional ways of praying:

1) To help keep the mind from wandering and being distracted in prayer, many devout pray-ers have used the *Centring prayer*. This focuses inwards by concentrating on a short 'breath prayer', used repeatedly. An example of this is the *Jesus prayer*: 'Lord Jesus Christ, Son of God, have mercy on me a sinner.' This moves my thoughts from my mind to my heart as I focus on Jesus. It is helpful when we want to quietly be with him in spirit, or even when doing routine tasks.[44]

2) Praying Scripture is a way we have found helpful in our devotions, using the Psalms or praying the Gospels. A well-known form of this is *Lectio Divina*, which has been described in modern terms by Joyce Huggett in her book *Open to God*. She calls the four steps (*Lectio*, *Meditatio*, *Oratio*, *Contemplatio*) the 'Four

R's': read, receive, respond and rest.[45] This is further elaborated in the section on meditation. Using the prayers in Paul's Epistles is helpful in learning the art of prayer.

3) Another way of using Scripture in prayer is to project oneself back into an actual Gospel story; this is known as *Ignatian prayer*. Imagine that you are part of the narrative, encountering Jesus by being one of the characters in the story or just an observer. This is a creative method of responding to Scripture, feeling the impact of Jesus in a new way and drawing something practical to apply to your life.

4) Scripture, other than narrative, can be used in personal application for our present situation by applying words spoken to people of another era and taking them as a message to us today (*Augustinian prayer*). For example, 'I have redeemed you. I have called you by name, you are mine.'[46] While originally meant for Israel, this statement can have powerful personal meaning for us in prayer today.

There are many ways of praying. Paul urges us to: 'Pray in the Spirit on all occasions with *all kinds of prayers* and requests.'[47] Certain personality types find some forms of prayer too restrictive. As we are all unique and different, we each find there are ways of prayer that seem more suited to us. 'There is no form of prayer that is best for everyone and for every given occasion.'[48] For some people their lives are their prayer, living and acting out a life with Jesus moment by moment. Many Christians like formal prayers and liturgy, while others prefer to use lists, limiting prayer to intercession. Those in a charismatic tradition include tongues, prophecy and healing in their praying.

Growth in our prayer life comes as we explore and use different ways of praying. Mark Virkler, in his book *Dialogue with God*, describes a form of prayer that can open our hearts, minds and spirits in a new and refreshing way.[49] (See the journalling section later.) In a workshop on prayer at our church we asked the participants to brainstorm in groups on 'Prayer is . . .' Figure 8.1 covers some of the ideas we came up with.

God's longing for us, his desire to draw us to himself and give us himself is greater than any desire we may have. We can trust his longing for us. He waits for our willingness.[50]

SOLITUDE

While we have seen that prayer is not always an individual exercise and is often a communal activity in the worship of a congregation or in a small group, growth to wholeness through prayer is an individual and personal journey. Jesus said, 'When you pray, go into your room, close the door.'[51] In other words, find a quiet, secluded and private place to be alone with God. Jesus prayed alone on the hillsides of Judea and Galilee, and drew strength for his mission from this.

Many of us are afraid to be alone. Some live in a family or community where the opportunity to be alone is not easy. In densely packed cities of this world it may be almost impossible to be physically alone. However, we can withdraw into ourselves even on a crowded bus or a busy street. What happens when we are alone? It is the best environment in which to face up to ourselves, especially when we meet God there. 'Solitude is the place where the whole of our personality and being is drawn together in the transforming presence of God's love.'[52] This is scary. I need courage to face God like this, but in solitude I hear him say, 'Fear not . . . draw near . . . come to me.' In that meeting, we not only discover God but confront ourselves. We come face to face with our poverty of spirit, human frailty, self-centredness, as well as our uniqueness and beauty.

Solitude is a necessary ingredient in our journey to

197

wholeness. Being an introvert, I (Agnes) enjoy solitude. This has not always been so as I grew up in a close family. I like being with people, and used people to fill those empty spaces of which I was afraid and unconsciously avoided. As an extrovert, I (John) enjoy people and they 'charge my batteries'. Over the past few years I have discovered the immense value of periods of solitude and silence, just to be with God and listen to him. Henri Nouwen wrote, 'Life without a quiet centre easily becomes destructive . . . In solitude we discover that our life is not a possession to be defended but a gift to be shared.'[53]

MEDITATION

Setting aside time for daily meditation is essential for growth in spiritual wholeness. Meditation is like medication – it may not result in instant cures, but given time to work will help recovery or maintain health. Christian meditation is thinking about God and actively using our imagination, reasoning, intellect, memory and will to discover what God is saying to us. Meditation is tuning in and listening with our minds so that our hearts will respond. It is focusing without distraction; detaching ourselves from other things so that our attention is absorbed in God.

The psalmist David mentions meditation in many of the psalms he wrote. His practice was to meditate day and night, sometimes all day long.[54] God reveals himself to us in three great books: the Scriptures, Nature and the events of our daily lives. David refers to these three sources for meditation: God's word, his wonders and his works.[55] Biblical meditation is the devotional practice of pondering on, delighting in and feeding on a portion of Scripture. David meditated on God's law given through Moses, but we have so much more Scripture to delight in. Do we make as much use of it as David did?

Over the entrance of the Museum in Christchurch, New Zealand, are words from the book of Job, 'Lo these are parts of his ways: but how little a portion is heard of him?'[56] Museums capture only a little of the wonder of God's world. We can never exhaust the extent of creation, meeting God in the minuteness of a tiny insect or the vastness of the universe. Psalm 19 is a classic example of meditation on both God's creation and his word. In Psalm 139, David meditates on the wonder of the intricate uniqueness of each one of us. In meditation we stop to look, to listen and to inhale; to feel, ponder and meet our God in new ways.

Meditation moves into *contemplation* as our thoughts turn from investigating to wondering. 'Meditation investigates; contemplation wonders.'[57] David reached this place: 'Be still and know that I am God.' 'For God alone my soul waits in silence.'[58] Contemplation transforms head-prayer into heart-prayer. Richard Foster calls it 'loving attentiveness to God',[59] not saying, asking or doing, but just being in God's presence. The practices of meditation and contemplation are powerful ways of leading us into, and helping us maintain, spiritual wholeness.

RETREATS

An engine needs tuning, a house needs refurbishing and clothes may need remodelling from time to time. In the same way, we do well to evaluate where we are on our spiritual journey. Thomas Merton said, 'Some people have to be alone before they can find their true selves.'[60] Retreats are best taken in short bursts initially, perhaps starting with a day and building up to longer times. They are not only good for reflective people and introverts, we all need spaces in our lives.

Silent retreats are wonderful times for solitude, even though you may be participating in the retreat with others. Just as plants bloom, seed and then rest, so humans need times just *to be*. Thinking of a retreat as 'a holiday with God' can change any apprehension into joyful anticipation. If you allow God to dictate the agenda on your retreat, anticipate the unexpected. He is the God of surprises.

Learning to become *open to him* is the key. Sometimes he brings painful awarenesses to mind that need to be dealt with, freeing us to continue our growth to wholeness. At these times God will provide the fortitude and desire to carry on. His promise is to be with us, even on occasions when we feel that he is absent. God wants to develop our faith and trust, which may not grow as well when we are more conscious of his presence. 'He is nearer to us when we are least aware of it.'[61] A retreat can be just a time to relax, enjoying the company of Jesus, as 'he leads us beside the still waters'.[62]

To discover more clearly what God is doing in our lives during a retreat, it helps to have someone to guide us. Most organised retreats provide spiritual directors to work daily with each retreatant, giving encouragement and support. The purpose of this exercise is to discover what the Holy Spirit is doing in our lives as we share together what is going on. This helps us to respond and go further in knowing Jesus.

JOURNALLING

We have emphasised that growth towards wholeness is a journey. A journal is a record of that journey and a valuable tool for plotting life's course. A diary is for planning and recording daily activities. By contrast, a journal is a personal record of thoughts, feelings, desires and goals; recording painful and joyous happenings. As you write, process what is going on in your life, search for meaning and ask questions, even those for which there may not be an obvious answer. It is a chance to reflect on and process unresolved issues.

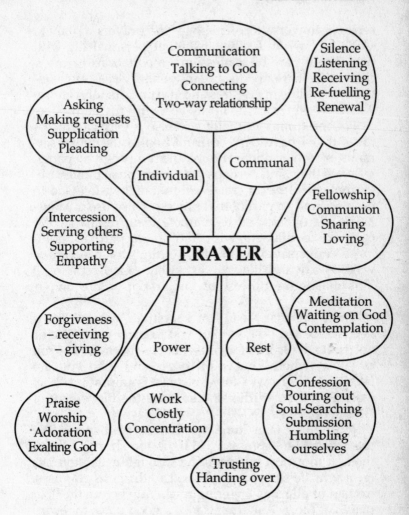

Figure 8.1. Aspects of prayer

Your journal records your own unique journey, not for others to share. Keep this writing in a special note-book, labelled PRIVATE. It is like a plot of land where trespassers are not welcome. My (Agnes) journal is a series of conversations, musings and prayers written to God. As I write, I share my inner personal life with him. There may be confessions, meditations or intercessions. I share my disappointments, release my emotions or outline my desires and dreams. As John Henry Newman expressed it, 'I pray best with my pen'.

For me (John) journalling is also a way to process ideas that I have derived from books, the Bible, sermons or conversations. I think them through on paper, redefine them and perhaps turn them into a prayer. My journal is a place for creative thinking, inviting God to be specifically a part of that process. I also use my journal to plan goals and re-evaluate them regularly. We both like to 'dialogue with God' in our journals, holding a conversation with him, writing down what we want to say and how we experience God replying.[63] This makes the process of 'inspiration' more understandable.

There are many ways of keeping a journal, but it needs to be the best way for you to meet your specific needs. It is a record of where you have been, where you are now, where you want to go, and who you are becoming. If growth to wholeness is important, how essential to record this and so trace the movement of God in our lives.

Journalling takes time, but is time well spent. 'We often hear the expression, "Life is too short". But we make it too short by travelling through it like tourists on a whistle-stop tour, satisfied with mere glimpses, instead of pilgrims lingering reverently before the holy places of life.'[64] A journal is also a good place to record and process dreams. (Further information on journalling, meditation and dreams is in our previous book, *Created for Intimacy*.[65])

DREAMS

Everyone dreams, but not everyone recalls their

dreams. Those who can remember and record dreams find them a rich resource to help their growth to wholeness. Dreams are couched in our own symbolic language. If we listen to them, they can give us useful information from our subconscious. Repetitive dreams are even more important. We struggle to unravel the meaning of our dreams, as famous characters like Pharoah and Nebuchadnezzar did in biblical times, but we have some modern 'Josephs' and 'Daniels' today who can help us interpret them.[66]

There are ways of understanding the symbols, language and people in our dreams, and we also need to take notice of the feelings that they give us. All details are important, however insignificant they may seem at the time. 'What is my dream saying?' may be better expressed, 'What questions is my dream asking me?' A separate journal can be used to record dreams. However, including them in your everyday journal means that you can see how they fit into the occurrences of your daily life. This helps to make the meaning clearer.

Dreams are an important way that God speaks to us, if we are prepared to listen. The Bible has over 200 references to dreams and visions. Together with their interpretation, this occupies a third of Scripture. Westerners are not as in tune with dreams as are people from other cultures, although there is a return to the appreciation of dreams following Carl Jung's work. Many modern scholars have also written about dreams, such as John Sanford, Morton Kelsey and Herman Riffel. Working with our dreams 'daily challenges us to come to consciousness about who we are, and how we are uniquely called by God along a path toward holiness and wholeness.'[67]

SPIRITUAL DIRECTION

Another aid to growth in spiritual wholeness is to have

regular spiritual direction. This is a different process from counselling. The counsellor helps people deal with problems and grow through the circumstances of their lives. The spiritual director helps directees discover what the Holy Spirit is doing in their life, exploring ways God is leading them on the path to wholeness. Each person is on their own unique journey, and the task of the spiritual director is to walk a part of that journey with them as a guide and companion. Together they endeavour to discover the right path, and pay attention to God.

Finding a Spiritual Director may not be easy, but there is a growing interest in this discipline among Christians of many denominations, and more people are being trained in this skill. If spiritual direction appeals to you, pray that the Lord will lead you to someone who is able to mentor you in your walk with God.

All of life, including their experience of prayer, provides the raw material from which to discover what God is saying and doing. Spiritual direction has been beautifully described as the work of a midwife, assisting the coming to birth and maturity of the new life.[68] Like a midwife, the director can see and hear the movements of the new life by watching, listening and trusting the process. Growth to spiritual wholeness involves waiting for our patient God who is never in a hurry. As a midwife, I (Agnes) am aware of the need for sensitivity and tact, to be supportive and encouraging during the painful birth process. Midwifery is focused work. So too, spiritual direction requires focused listening and a clear awareness of the process. Paul refers to sharing in 'the pains of childbirth until Christ is formed in you'.[69]

The seven pathways we have touched on here cover some of the essentials for growth to spiritual wholeness. These deal with the core of who we are, our spirituality. If our centre is not whole, we will try to find our identity in what is peripheral: work, money, our 'toys', the body, sex, drugs, a person or even religion. If our centre is whole, and is a place where we are secure, we can relate to these external things in a healthy, balanced way. 'God is not glorified in half persons. The more we open ourselves to life, to let the waves of life flow over us, allowing ourselves to feel, to suffer and to wonder, the more we are opening ourselves to God.'[70]

SUMMARY

Because we have been created spiritual beings, spiritual wholeness is something we all desire. There are many false trails, but there are also some well-established pathways for finite human beings to make a real relationship with an infinite God and grow to wholeness.

REFLECTIONS AND EXERCISES

1) Describe in your journal or to your group your own discovery of God. Was it a dramatic or gradual experience?

2) Which of the false trails described have you been down? Are there any others that have enticed you? What brought you back onto the right path to God?

3) Study the aspects of prayer listed in Figure 8.1. Which of these can you identify with? Discuss them in your group or with a friend.

4) Are you able to build periods of solitude into your life? Reflect on ways that you could do so, and how to increase these times. Plan for this.

5) Write out a recent dream with as much detail as you can remember.

- How does it relate to your current circumstances?
- What feelings were you left with?
- What do you think the symbols or people in your dream stand for?
- Have you any clues to its meaning, or what God might be saying to you?
- Pray about this.
- Talk it over with someone who understands dreams.

6) Choose a short passage of Scripture, such as a Psalm, a verse from Isaiah, a saying of Jesus, or part of the Gospel narrative. Spend several minutes absorbing its meaning, and what Jesus might be saying to you through it. Try the Four R's method (see p 195).

7) Take a slow walk through a park, the Botanical Gardens, some bush or forest, a field or along a beach. Become absorbed and awed by the wonder of God's creation.

• Then write your reflections about this experience.

NINE

TOWARDS WHOLENESS
AND MATURITY

The glory of God is a human being who is fully alive.
St Irenaeus[1]

'Are you not thirsty?', said the Lion.

'I'm *dying* of thirst', said Jill.

'Then drink', said the Lion.

'May I – could I – would you mind going away while I do?' said Jill.

The Lion answered this only by a look and a very low growl . . . The delicious rippling noise of the stream was driving her nearly frantic.

'Will you promise not to – do anything to me if I do come?' said Jill.

'I make no promise,' said the Lion.

Jill was so thirsty now that, without noticing it, she had come a step nearer.

'*Do* you eat girls?' she said.

'I have swallowed up girls and boys, women and men, kings and emperors, cities and realms,' said the Lion . . .

'I daren't come and drink,' said Jill.

'Then you will die of thirst,' said the Lion.

'Oh, dear!' said Jill, coming another step nearer. 'I suppose I must go and look for another stream, then.'

'There is no other stream,' said the Lion.
C.S. Lewis[2]

The journey to wholeness and maturity can be scary. Wholeness is like the sparkling water that Jill in the Chronicles of Narnia wanted so much. However, as Jill discovered, to achieve what we want involves taking some risks. Wholeness may require making radical changes in our physical lifestyle. It will certainly mean reviewing and renewing our minds, and adjusting our values. If I am 'emotionally illiterate', I will have to learn new ways of relating to people in order to experience intimacy. Social wholeness means moving from a life of self-focus to becoming other-centred. To strive for spiritual wholeness challenges the very core of our being. 'Christianity is not about being secure in the middle, but being available and vulnerable on the edge.'[3]

Becoming a whole person is somewhat like the change a butterfly experiences after emerging from its chrysalis. When its wings are dry, it has to use them to explore a totally new environment. The butterfly is now much more vulnerable than it was in the safety of its hard chrysalis. However, it is free to become the beautiful creature it was created to be.

As we have seen throughout the book, Tony and Jan had to 'spread their wings' and take some risks. They started by making significant changes to their physical lifestyle. Then they altered their goals and communication pattern. This led to a desire to become other-centred, trying to meet each other's needs rather than focusing on their own. They began listening to one another's feelings and stopped dumping their anger on each other. So their intimacy grew. Eventually, they started to share their spiritual desires and help each other to grow in this dimension. When we last talked to them, they realised that they had not 'arrived', but they were committed to a journey of growth in personal and relationship wholeness.

EXPANDING SPHERES OF WHOLENESS

There are three important spheres of wholeness in human society. They overlap, interact, and move from the centre outwards. (See Figure 9.1.)

1. Personal Wholeness

Most of what we have been saying throughout this book is aimed at developing individual wholeness. It must start there, with an awareness of our deficiencies, and a desire to grow and mature. The journey to wholeness is a *lifelong process*. Writing this book has stimulated us to review and challenge ourselves in all aspects of our own growth, and has been a humbling experience. It has given us a desire to only preach what we practise, rather than just practise what we preach. Unless we grow in personal wholeness, we cannot be effective in other spheres of wholeness.

2. Relationship Wholeness

Growth to wholeness is not merely for individual benefit. It begins there. As we grow to become whole people ourselves, we can relate in more healthy ways to others. Whole people are able to forget about themselves and be *other-centred*. However, in a desire for wholeness there is always the danger of self-preoccupation, which is counter-productive.

The Dead Sea is 400 metres below sea level; the Jordan River constantly flows into it, pouring in over 500 million cubic metres of water a year, but no water flows out again. In that intense desert heat, the water evaporates and leaves behind increasing deposits of salt, sulphur and other minerals. As a result, no fish or birds can live there. It is a place of death.

The Red Sea is only about 200 kilometres away, but by contrast, it teems with fish and all kinds of life. What is the difference? The Red Sea receives even more

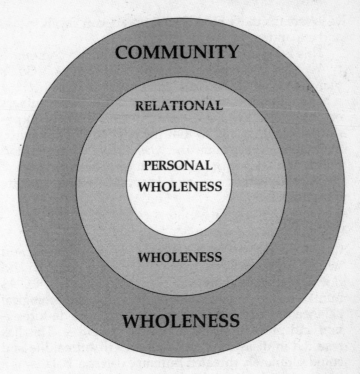

Figure 9.1. Expanding spheres of wholeness

water but it also passes it on. So in life, if we focus only on ourselves, we will stagnate and die. On the other hand, if we share who we are and who we are becoming with others, we will continue to grow individually and in our relationships.

3. Community Wholeness

Communities are made up of individuals, and the health of the community reflects the wholeness of the individuals within it. As individuals work for wholeness within themselves and in their relationships, so the health of society will improve. A small amount of yeast affects the whole loaf of bread, causing it to rise and expand.[4]

This is an important concept in a church community. We saw in the last chapter how wholeness is God's plan for us as individuals: 'to become mature (*telios* = whole), attaining to the whole measure of the fullness of Christ.' But this is expressed in the context of corporate wholeness: '. . . so that the *body* of Christ may be built up . . . From him the *whole body* . . . grows and builds itself up in love, as each part does its work.'[5] Individual wholeness and corporate wholeness are inseparable.

BALANCE

One of the principles of nature is balance: summer and winter, night and day, sea and dry land, tidal ebb and flow, interaction between plant and animal life. As human beings have exploited the earth, the ecological balance has been upset through pollution, de-forestation and plundering other natural resources. This has resulted in disastrous consequences to animal life and could ultimately threaten human existence. Balance is a *key factor* in developing wholeness. In Chapter One, we described an unbalanced person as someone who may be an intellectual genius yet socially or emotionally immature; physically fit but lacking spiritual development.

Others focus on spiritual growth, but fail to develop healthy relationships. Mature, whole people are growing in all five areas of their lives. Some parts may be more developed than others, but no aspect of their lives is neglected.

Balance is necessary in the emphasis we place on the physical, intellectual, emotional, social and spiritual areas of our lives, and in their relationship to one another. Balance is also required within each part. Solomon said, 'There is a time for everything, and a season for every activity under heaven.'[6] The following outline summarises this principle.

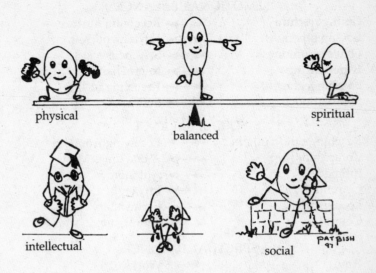

Figure 9.2. Maintaining the balance

PHYSICAL BALANCE

Calories in (dietary intake)	⟷ Calories out (exercise)
Work	⟷ Relaxation
Waking	⟷ Sleeping
Separateness	⟷ Touch

MENTAL BALANCE

Left brain activity	⟷ Right brain activity
Reason	⟷ Imagination
Talking	⟷ Listening
Seriousness	⟷ Fun and humour
Vertical, logical thinking	⟷ Lateral, creative thinking
Positive thinking	⟷ Realistic evaluation
Thinking	⟷ Feeling
Logic	⟷ Intuition
Analysis	⟷ Synthesis
Knowledge	⟷ Wisdom

EMOTIONAL BALANCE

Giving nurture	←→ Receiving nurture
Loving others	←→ Loving yourself
Other-centredness	←→ Self-focus
Experiencing	←→ Internalising
Sharing feelings	←→ Receiving feelings
Stimulation	←→ Stillness

SOCIAL BALANCE

Reaching out to others	←→ Receiving from others
Companionship	←→ Alone times
Intimacy	←→ Autonomy
Community	←→ Privacy
Leadership	←→ Partnership
Control	←→ Submission

SPIRITUAL BALANCE

Faith	←→ Works
Grace	←→ Law
Worship	←→ Service
Doctrine	←→ Parable and metaphor
Celebration	←→ Meditation

OVERALL BALANCE

Eternity	←→ Time
'Kairos'	←→ 'Chronos'
BEING	←→ DOING

Figure 9.3. Balancing the opposites

SUMMARY OF THE JOURNEY TO WHOLENESS

Growth towards wholeness begins with a *decision* to aim for maturity. Nothing will happen until we make a conscious choice to grow in all areas of our being. Not choosing to grow is in fact a decision to choose the opposite. We have covered many aspects of the journey to wholeness: physical, intellectual, emotional, social and spiritual. It is clearly impossible to tackle all of these fully at once, but we can make a start in one area. Because human nature is indivisible, progress in one department can encourage growth in other parts of our lives.

It is important to develop in a *balanced* way. To be growing mentally but neglecting our physical bodies, or to be spiritually mature and yet socially inept is a distortion of wholeness. Obviously, individuals differ in their personalities, gifts and interests, and some aspects of the life of a whole person may be more developed than others. However, neglect of any aspect of who we are will spoil our wholeness.

Figure 9.4 is an overview or map of aspects of wholeness discussed in this book. Maps can show us where we have come from, where we are, and how to reach a desired destination. They can be very helpful, but we learn more about the road by actually travelling on it than by consulting even the best map. This chapter ends our brief study of wholeness. We trust it will be the beginning of a journey to wholeness for some, and for others an encouragement to continue a journey already begun. One traveller put it this way: 'Forgetting what is behind and straining towards what is ahead, I press on towards the goal to win the prize for which God has called me heavenwards in Christ Jesus.'[7]

CELEBRATE LIFE

Life is to be lived to the full, so say 'YES' to life. 'Celebration brings joy into life and joy makes us strong.'[8] Joyful celebration follows when all areas of our lives are being transformed and are growing towards their potential. Jesus said that he wanted his joy to be in us, so that our joy might be complete.[9] Joy is infectious, not only to other people but also for ourselves. It counteracts a tendency to anxiety and depression. Joy is a choice, and celebration a decision. Celebration helps to restore a sense of balance to life, gives us perspective and sharpens our vision.

We have all been created to become whole people,

each in her or his unique way. Paul said: 'I keep working towards that day when I will finally be all that Christ saved me for and wants me to be.'[10] Wherever you are on your journey to wholeness, there is more to be discovered. Only lack of vision limits our progress, so *go for the big dream*.

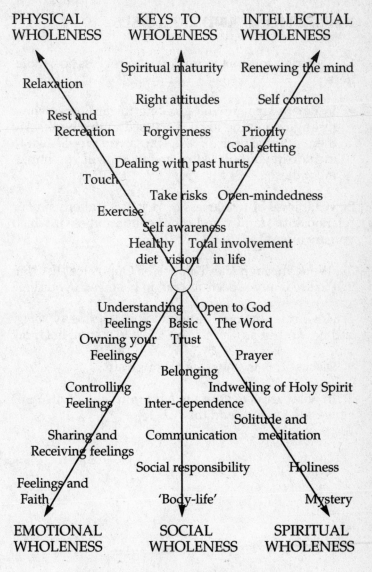

Figure 9.4. Aspects of wholeness

REFLECTIONS AND EXERCISES

1) Describe in your journal your progress to wholeness.

• In what ways are you growing towards wholeness through applying ideas discussed in this book? Are there other aspects of wholeness you would like to include in your life? How and when will you implement these?

2) What level of wholeness or lack of it is there in your relationships, family and other communities of which you are a part?

3) Work through the 'Balance of Opposites' list (Fig 9.3) to see if any aspects are not in balance in your life?

4) How much of your life would you describe as *'doing'* and how much as *'being'*? Are these in a good balance?

• Discuss this in your journal or group.

5) In what areas of your life have you said a full 'Yes'? How could you extend this?

RELAXATION EXERCISES

1) Relaxation Breathing

Anatomy of respiration. The main muscle involved in breathing is the diaphragm, which is a strong dome-shaped muscle below the heart and lungs. It is attached to the lower ribs all around the chest, and separates the thorax from the abdomen. The oesophagus and large blood vessels pass through the centre of it, but the rest of the dome is muscle. It works like bellows, so that when the diaphragm moves down, air is drawn into the lungs. At the same time, this movement displaces the liver and intestines downwards, forcing the tummy forwards. When the diaphragm relaxes, the abdominal muscles push in the opposite direction, forcing air out of the lungs as the abdominal contents are pushed upwards. (See Figure 1.) Rib and neck muscles play a smaller part in respiration. As they lift the upper part of the chest, this can increase the volume of air a further fifteen per cent. But these muscles are not used in relaxation breathing.

Relaxation breathing. Tense breathing is rapid and shallow, using only the upper parts of the lungs. Relaxation breathing is the opposite: slow and deep, using the diaphragm. Relaxation can be induced in the body by

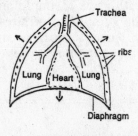
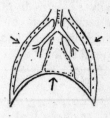

BREATHING IN   BREATHING OUT

Figure 1.   The process of respiration

diaphragmatic breathing. The speed of your breathing can be judged by counting at one second intervals in your mind as you take a breath. The normal breathing rate is about four seconds per breath (fifteen a minute). Aim to slow your breathing down to about two or three breaths a minute during this exercise.

Lie down on a firm surface such as a carpet, and make yourself comfortable with a small pillow under your head or lower back, if necessary. Shut your eyes, and start by listening to your normal breathing and tuning in to its rhythm. Then gradually change it by drawing deeper and slower breaths. Breathe in on a count of seven, and out on eight counts. Breathe as slowly as is comfortable for you initially, and then train yourself to breathe even more slowly. You can rest a hand on your abdomen to ensure you are using your diaphragm. Each time you breathe out, tell yourself to 'relax and let go'. Each time you relax, do it a little more deeply. Practice this for five or ten minutes twice a day.

After a few week's practice, you will only need to take about three deep breaths to become fully relaxed. You can do this standing up, sitting back in a chair, or wherever you are. Stopping for a minute to breathe this way several times a day can prevent a build up of tension in stressful situations. Even when doing aerobic exercises, you will find that your breathing will be much more diaphragmatic once you have learned this skill. Deep, diaphragmatic breathing is a simple and effective way of controlling the symptoms of stress, such as rapid heart beat, sweats, panic sensations and headaches. Better still, it can prevent them from developing.

2) Muscle Relaxation

The easiest way to learn this skill is to lie on your back on a firm surface. Start off with a few deep breaths, using your diaphragm. Then forget about your breathing and focus on your muscles. Visualise your muscles, group by group, and tell them to relax. Start with your fingers . . . hands . . . forearms . . . upper arms . . . shoulders . . . muscles between the shoulder-blades. Then focus on the back of your neck . . . scalp . . . forehead . . . eyebrows . . . face . . . lips . . . tongue . . . jaw . . . front of your neck.

Take another slow deep breath, and as you breathe out, relax your chest muscles. Relax your spinal muscles, start at the top and work all the way down, telling the muscles to relax. They will. Relax your abdominal muscles . . . hips . . . thighs . . . calf . . . muscles . . . ankles . . . feet . . . toes. Let your whole body feel limp, just like a rag doll, as if you could not move. Let all the tension go and enjoy the delicious warm feeling of total relaxation. No movement, no tension, just relaxation. You're in charge of your body now, not the other way round. After a minute or two, repeat the process, working up from toes to scalp this time. Focus on any muscle group that is still a little tense.

The old method was to tense up your muscles each time before relaxing them. This may help at the beginning, in order to feel the difference between tension and relaxation. But to keep doing this throughout the exercise wastes half the time. Just focus on relaxing your muscles.

3) Use Your Imagination

Imagine that you are lying on a sandy beach. Take time to *feel* the warm sand underneath you . . . the sun shining on your face and body . . . the gentle breeze. *Listen* to the lapping of the waves . . . the cry of sea-gulls. *See* the blue sky and tiny white clouds . . . the sparkling water. *Smell* the salt air and seaweed. Become part of the scene. Enjoy the beauty of God's creation, and bask in this pleasurable experience. Enjoy the feeling of total relaxation a little longer. Then take two slow deep breaths and stretch all your muscles. Open your eyes and feel refreshed, energised and relaxed. (If you do not like a beach scene, create a 'favourite place' of your own.)

Do this exercise for ten minutes twice a day, (at least five minutes of breathing and five minutes of muscle relaxation). Choose a time in the day when you are not feeling totally exhausted, because if you are very tired, this exercise could send you to sleep. The purpose is not to induce sleep but produce relaxation. If you do it at a time when you are not too tired, you will feel refreshed and energised. It takes about three weeks to learn a new habit. This is a good one that you can use for a lifetime.

NOTES AND REFERENCES

Chapter One – 'Wholth'

1) Seneca, Roman philosopher, orator, statesman, 4 BC to AD 65, from *Epistulae ad Lucilium*, Epis LXXVI, Section III.
2) The term 'wholth' was coined by Dr Beryl Howie as a description of 'wholistic health'.
3) M. Scott Peck, *Further Along the Road Less Travelled* (New York: Simon & Schuster, 1993) p 17.
4) Galatians 6:4; 2 Corinthians 10:12.
5) D. Gareth Jones, *Our Fragile Brain: A Christian Perspective on Brain Research* (Downer Grove: IVP, 1981) p 39.
6) Pierre Teilhard de Chardin, 1881–1955, French philosopher, theologian, palaeontologist.
7) Eknath Gaswaran, *Gandhi, the Man*, 2nd Edition (Nilgiri Press, 1978) p 145.
8) Plato, 427–348 BC. Greek philospher, scientist, writer, who together with Socrates and Aristotle laid the foundations of Western culture.
9) Travis, J and Ryan, R., *The Wellness Workbook: Creating Vibrant Health* (Berkeley: Ten Speed Press, 1981) p 2.
10) Fries, J & Capo, L, *Vitality and Aging* (San Francisco: Freeman Publishers, 1981).
11) Maslow, A.H., *Toward a Psychology of Being* (New York: Van Nostrand Reinhold, 1968) p 160.
12) Maslow, ibid, p 155.
13) For a classic exploration of this dilema, see Romans chapter 7.
14) V. Frankl, *Man's Search for Meaning* (New York: Simon & Schuster, revised, 1984).
15) Ibid., p 110.
16) Ibid., pp 115–118.
17) W. Glasser, *Reality Therapy* (New York: Harper & Row, 1969).
18) Albert Ellis, *Reason and Emotion in Psychology* (New York: Lyle Stuart, 1962).
19) H. Clinebell, *Growth Counselling for Marriage Enrichment* (Philadelphia: Fortess Press, 1975) p 2.
20) *'shlemut'*, which is derived from and related to *'shalom'* is the precise Hebrew word used to describe this extended meaning of shalom.
21) John 14:27; Philippians 4:7.
22) Luke 6:38 See also Ecclesiastes 11:1 (especially GNB).

23) John 20:19, 26.
24) Matthew 5:9; see also James 3:17,18.
25) Hillel, *Ethics of the Fathers*, Mishna 12 of Chapter 1.
26) We are grateful to Don Reekie (Presbyterian minister, Group Psychotherapist, Auckland) for these thoughts on contrasting *'shalom'* and *'sheol'*.
27) John 10:10.
28) See Mark 5:34; 6:56; Luke 8:48; 17:19; James 5:15.
29) Luke 10:25–37. See also Matthew 22:37–40 (emphasis ours)
30) John 8:46; 2 Corinthians 5:21; Hebrews 4:15.
31) Luke 2:52 (emphasis ours).
32) Matthew 5:48.
33) Ephesians 4:13; Romans 8:29.
34) Colossians 1:28, 29.
35) 1 Corinthians 14:20; 1 Peter 2:2; Hebrews 6:1 (emphasis ours).
36) Romans 12:1,2 (emphasis ours).
37) Ephesians 4:23, 24; 2 Timothy 2:15.
38) 2 Corinthians 10:5.
39) James 4:8.
40) 1 Corinthians 12:25; Colossians 1:28.
41) Romans 12:15; Galatians 6:2; Philippians 2:4.
42) Philippians 1:6.
43) Philippians 1:7.
44) John 5:1–15.
45) Charles Sherlock, *The Doctrine of Humanity* (Leicester: InterVarsity Press, 1996) p 219.
46) 1 Corinthians 13:12.

Chapter Two – 'Illth'

1) T.S. Eliot, poet, playwright, 1888–1965.
2) S. Covey & R. Merrill, *First Things First* (New York: Simon & Schuster, 1994) pp 15–16.
3) This concept is explored by Alvin Toffler in *Future Shock* (London: Pan, 1970).
4) T. Holmes & R. Rahe, 'The Social Readjustment Rating Scale' (*Journal of Psychosomatic Research*, Vol. 11, 1967) pp 213–218.
5) Gary Collins, *Your Magnificent Mind* (Grand Rapids: Baker, 1985) p 56.
6) Galatians 6:4; see also 2 Corinthians 10:12.
7) Psalm 127:1. It is clear that this psalm is not about building houses but lives and families.
8) 1 Corinthians 3:10–15.
9) Tim Hansel, *When I Relax I Feel Guilty* (Elgin: David Cook, 1979) explores workaholism and how to escape from it.
10) Frank Minirth and Paul Meier, *et al.*, *The Workaholic and His*

Family (Grand Rapids: Baker, 1981) especially Chapter 3.

11) Romans 15:1–3.

12) Galatians 1:10; 2 Corinthians 5:9 (TLB).

13) This concept of the 'drama triangle' was first described by Stephen Karpman in *Transactional Analysis Bulletin 36* (April 1968) pp 35–43.

14) For further reading on co-dependency, see two books giving opposing perspectives:

a) Melodie Beattie, *Codependent No More* (New York: Harper and Row, 1987).

b) J. Katz & A. Liu, *The Codependency Conspiracy* (New York: Time Werner, 1991).

15) Galatians 6:2 and 5 (GNB). In verse 2, the Greek word for burden is *baros*, which means the heavy load a slave might carry. In verse 5 the word for load is *portion*, or pack. Each soldier is required to carry his own pack, though may be called upon at times to help others.

16) M. Friedman & R. Roseman, *Type A Behaviour and Your Heart* (New York: Fawcett, Crest Books, 1978).

17) James Lynch, *The Language of the Heart* (New York: Basic Books, 1985).

18) M. Friedman & D. Ulmer, *Treating Type 'A' Behaviour and Your Heart* (London: Guild, 1985). This book outlines an excellent programme for changing Type-A behaviour.

19) Hans Selye, *The Stress of Life*, revised edition (New York: McGraw-Hill, 1976) p 74.

20) James 1:2–4; 12; Hebrews 12:11; Romans 5:3,4.

21) R. & J. Glasser, 'Stress-Associated Depression in Cellular Immunity', *Brain, Behaviour and Immunity* 1, 1987.

22) a) S. Cohen, *et al.*, 'Psychological Stress and Susceptibility to the Common Cold' *New England Journal of Medicine 325*, 1991.

b) Clover, R. *et al.*, 'Family Functioning and Stress as Predictors of Influenza B Influenza', *Journal of Family Practice 28*, May 1989.

23) B. McEwan & E. Stellar, 'Stress and the Individual Mechanisms Leading to Disease', *Archives of Internal Medicine 153*, Sept 27, 1993.

24) Paul Brand & Philip Yancey, *Pain: the Gift Nobody Wants* (New York: HarperCollins, 1993).

25) 1 Kings:18, 19.

26 Archibald Hart, Theology, News and Notes (*Fuller Theological Seminary Alumni Vol XXXI*, Number 1, March 1984) p 6.

27) Matthew 16:25; Mark 8:35; Luke 9:24; 17:33; John 12:25.

28) John 5:35.

29) See Luke 12:35 – 'Be dressed ready for service and keep your lamps burning.'

In Psalm 18:28 – David asked God to keep his lamp burning.

Chapter Three – Blocks and Keys

1) Matthew 7:13–14.
2) Proverbs 29:18 (KJV).
3) Mark 9:42.
4) J. & A. Sturt, *Created for Love* (Guildford: Eagle, 1994).
5) A proverb by the Chinese philosopher, Lau-tzu, made famous by Mau Tse Tung at the start of 'the long march' in 1934.
6) Hebrews 12:15.
7) Hope Edelman, *Motherless Daughters* (London: Hodder & Stoughton, 1994) p 103.
8) Matthew 5:4.
9) Paul Tournier, *The Meaning of Persons* (London: SCM Press, 1957).
10) John Powell explores the pull of our comfort zones in *The Christian Vision* (Allen, Texas, Argus, 1984) pp 35, 36, 82.
11) M. Louise Haskins. Quoted by King George VI in a speech at the height of World War II.
12) Margaret Magdelen, *Keeping a Spiritual Journal*, edited by Edward England (Godalming: Highland Books, 1991) p 95.
13) Exodus 21:24; Matthew 5:38.
14) Hancock and Mains, (Godalming: Highland, 1988) p 65. See also Romans 12:19.
15) David Augsburger, *The Freedom of Forgiveness* (Chicago: Moody, 1970) p 42.
16) Matthew 18:21,22.
17) Matthew 6:12, 14.
18) William James, 1842–1910, American philosopher and psychologist.
19) St Augustine of Hippo, *Confessions*, Book 1, Chapter 1.

Chapter Four – Physical Wholeness

1) Sophocles, Greek playwright, 496–406 BC.
2) A. Maslow, *Motivation and Personality*, 2nd ed. (New York: Harper & Row, 1970).
3) Nadine Wolf, *The Beauty Myth* (London: Vintage, 1990).
4) Psalm 139:14 (Jerusalem Bible).
5) Dr Deepak Chopra, *Ageless Body, Timeless Mind* (New York: Harmony Books, 1993) p 9.
6) Genesis 1:25; 31.
7) John 1:14; Galatians 4:4; 1 Timothy 3:16; 1 John 4:2.
8) *Evangelical Dictionary of Biblical Theology*, ed. W. Eltwell (Baker, 1996) p 72.
9) Genesis 2:7 KJV (emphasis ours).
10) H. Wheeler Robinson, 'Hebrew Psychology', in *The People and*

the Book, ed. Arthur Peake (Oxford: Clarendon, 1952) p 362.

11) Romans 7:18 (KJV 'our flesh').

12) 1 Corinthians 6:13,20 cp Romans 8:8.

13) 1 Corinthians 6:19; 2 Corinthians 6:16.

14) Romans 6:12,13 cp Galatians 5:17.

15) J.A.T. Robinson, *The Body* (London: ACP Press, 1966) p 31.

16) 1 Corinthians 9:27 (KJV).

17) 1 Corinthians 15:44ff. See John 20, 21.

18) Hippocrates, 460–377 BC, a Greek physician and teacher whose sound philosophical approach to medicine and life was enshrined in the Hippocratic Oath. Aristotle called him 'the great physician'.

19) Body fat is measured more accurately by the Body Mass Index, which is the weight (in kilograms) divided by the height 2 (in metres).

20) This chart is modified from J. Garrow, *Treat Obesity Seriously* (London: Churchill, 1981).

21) Michael Jansen, *The Vitamin Revolution in Health Care* (Greenville: Arcadia, 1996) p 95.

22) Nathan Pritikin, *The Pritikin Programme for Diet and Exercise* (New York: Bantam, 1980).

23) There is a range of nutritional supplements available, either as tablets or in powder form.

24) One useful book on this is *Vitamin C, The Master Nutrient*, by Sylvia Goodman (Connecticut:, Keats, 1991).

25) Free radicals are high-energy particles that have a single (unpaired) electron in the outer ring of their molecule. They can damage the body tissues in their search for another electron, especially free radicals derived from oxygen. They disrupt the normal production of DNA, alter lipids in cell membranes, destroy nutrients and lead to premature aging, heart disease and cancer. We are exposed to free radicals through radiation; ultra violet light; cigarette smoke; eating processed foods, charred or burned foods; exposure to toxic chemicals and heavy metals in food and water.

26) Michael Jansen, op. cit. pp 65–69.

27) Ashley Montague, *Touching* (New York: Harper & Row, 1971) p 4.

28) Ibid, p 2, cites research showing that a human embryo of about six weeks will respond to touch.

29) Jules Older, *Touching is Healing* (New York: Stein & Day, 1982). This book provides an excellent review of some of this research, and the battle to change the prevailing belief that children should be touched as little as possible.

30) Virginia Satir, Family Therapist and author of *People Making* (Palo Alto: Science and Behaviour, 1972).

31) Jesus often touched *children* (Mark 10:13–16); the *sick* (Mark 1:41; 7:33; 8:22–25; Luke: 4:40; 13:13; 22:51); even the *dead* (Mark 5:41; Luke 7:14); and especially his *friends* (John 13:23–25).

32) See Hebrews 6:2; Acts: 6:6; 8:17; 9:17; 13:3; 19:6; 28:8; 2 Timothy 1:6; James 5:14; 1 Peter 5:14.

33) Richard Foster, *Celebration of Discipline* (London: Hodder & Stoughton, 1980) p 20.

34) P. Meier, F. Minirth, F. Wichern, *Introduction to Psychology and Counselling* (Grand Rapids: Baker, 1982) p 198.

35) Herman Riffel, *Your Dreams: God's Neglected Gift* (Lincoln: Chosen Books, 1981)
Morton Kelsey, *Dreams: A Way to Listen to God* (New York: Paulist Press, 1982).

36) Exodus 20:8–11; Mark 2:27.

37) Robert Louis Stevenson, 1850–1894.

Chapter Five – Intellectual Wholeness

1) Marcus Aurelius, AD 121–180, Roman philosopher, writer, emperor from 161.

2) *The Mind and Brain* (Amsterdam: Time-Life Books, 1993) p 10.

3) Wilder Penfield, *The Mystery of the Mind* (Princeton: University Press, 1975) pp 96, 87.

4) Gary R. Collins, *Your Magnificent Mind* (Grand Rapids: Baker, 1988).

5) R. W. Sperry, 'The Great Cerebral Commissure', *Scientific American* (January 1964).

6) M. Kinsbourne, 'Sad Hemisphere, Happy Hemisphere', *Psychology Today*, Vol 15, 1981.

7) Albert Einstein, 1879–1955, renowned physicist who developed the theory of relativity and was awarded the Nobel prize in 1921.

8) Archimedes, 290–212 BC, Greek mathematician and inventor. (The principle he discovered was that a solid, denser than a fluid, when immersed in that fluid will be lighter by the weight of the amount of fluid displaced, showing why ships float.)

9) Ecclesiates 9:10. Go for the big dream! See Isaiah 54:2.

10) Colossians 3:23.

11) Proverbs 11:24, 25. See also Psalm 112:5.

12) Richard Foster, *Celebration of Discipline* (London: Hodder & Stoughton, 1983) p 79.

13) Luke 6:38.

14) Philippians 2:4.

15) Proverbs 29:18 (KJV).

16) Emil Coué, French pharmacist and psychotherapist, 1857–1926.

17) C. Stone & N. Hill, *Success Through Positive Mental Attitude*

(Englewood Cliffs: Prentice-Hall, 1960).

18) N.V. Peale, *The Power of Positive Thinking* (Oxford: OUP, 1994).

19) N.V. Peale, *You Can if You Think You Can* (Englewood Cliffs: Prentice-Hall, 1974) p 199.

20) V. Frankl, *Man's Search for Meaning* (New York: Simon & Schuster, revised, 1984).

21) See Psalm 25:5(b); 147:11; Ephesians 1:18; Hebrews 6:19; 11:1.

22) C. Peterson *et al.*, *Learned Helplessness: A Theory for the Age of Personal Control* (New York: Oxford University Press, 1993).

23) Philippians 4:8.

24) J. Levin, 'Humour and Mental Health', *Encyclopedia of Mental Health*, Vol 3 (New York: Franklin Watts, 1963) pp 786–799.

25) Proverbs 17:22 (GNB).

26) See Matthew 13:3, 10, 13, 34, 35, 53.

27) '*yetser*', is used four times in the Bible; twice of evil imagination: Genesis 6:5; 8:21 (AV) and twice positively: 1 Chronicles 29:18 and Isaiah 26:3.

28) Isaiah 26:3.

29) 1 Timothy 6:6.

30) Philippians 4:11–12.

31) Hyman Judah Schactel.

32) Gary Collins, op. cit. p. 56.

33) Joel 2:28; Acts 2:17.

34) Steven Covey, *The Seven Habits of Highly Effective People* (New York: Simon and Schuster, 1989).

35) S.R. Covey & A.R. Merrill, *First Things First* (New York: Simon & Schuster, 1994).

36) Ibid, p 146.

37) See James 1:3–5; 1 Peter 1:6–7.

38) Matthew 6:25–34.

39) See Psalm 55:22; 1 Peter 5:7.

40) Galatians 5:22.

41) 1 Thessalonians 5:6–8; 2 Timothy 1:7; Titus 2:1–12.

42) 1 Peter 1:13; 4:7; 5:8; 2 Peter 1:6.

43) John 8:32 (emphasis ours).

44) Romans 12:2.

45) 1 Corinthians 2:14–16. See also Romans 8:6.

46) H. Blamires, *The Christian Mind* (London: SPCK, 1963) p 45.

47) 2 Corinthians 10:4–5. For a further explanation of this process, see Chapter 6 of *Created for Love* (Guildford: Eagle, 1994).

48) 2 Timothy 3:16; John 16:13; 1 Corinthians 2:14–15.

49) John 14:15–17; 16:13.

50) Ephesians 4:22–23 (emphasis ours).

Chapter Six – Emotional Wholeness

1) John Powell, *Fully Human, Fully Alive* (Valencia: Tabor, 1976) p 9.

2) D. Goleman, *Emotional Intelligence* (London: Bloomsbury, 1996) p 36.

3) Archibald Hart, *Unlocking the Mystery of Your Emotions* (Dallas: Word, 1989) p ix.

4) Paul Ekman, 'An Argument for the Basic Emotions' (*Cognition and Emotions*, 1992).

5) Stanley Schater, 'The Interaction of Cognitive and Physiological Determinants of Emotional State', *Social Psychology*, Vol 1 (New York: Academic Press, 1964).

6) The Stoic movement was started in Athens by Zeno about 300 BC. They stressed reason, acceptance and mental tranquility (akin to apathy). They taught that being moved by emotions indicated an unhealthy mind. A blend of Stoicism and Platonism is reflected in the writings of the Church Fathers.

7) Brian Knight, *Your Feelings Are Your Friends* (Auckland: Hodder & Stoughton, 1978). A helpful book on understanding, accepting and using your feelings.

8) Galen, AD 129–199, distinguished Greek physician, anatomist and philosopher who founded experimental physiology. His teaching influenced medicine for the next 1,400 years.

9) Proverbs 17:22. See Proverbs 15:13,15.

10) H. Friedman & S. Boothby-Kewley, 'The Disease-Prone Personality: A Meta-Analytic View' (*American Psychologist* 42, 1987).

11) D. Goleman, op. cit., Chapter 11.

12) Sharing and receiving feelings is explored in *Created for Intimacy* (Guildford: Eagle, 1996) Chapter 7.

13) Ephesians 4:15 (emphasis ours).

14) Brian & Lynda Jones, *Men Have Feelings Too* (Wheaton: Victor, 1988) p 159.

15) D. & V. Mace, *How To Have a Happy Marriage* (Nashville: Abingdon, 1978) pp 113, 114.

16) Aristotle, 384–322 BC. He followed Socrates and Plato, as one of the three great Greek philosophers.

17) Examples of 'righteous anger': Exodus 32:19; Mark 3:5; Romans 2:5–8. Examples of 'unrighteous anger': Genesis 4:5–8; Numbers 22:27; Jonah 4:1–4.

18) S.K. Mallick & B.R. McCandless, 'A Study of Catharsis in Aggression', *Journal of Personality and Social Psychology* 4 (1966).

19) R. Williams, *The Trusting Heart* (New York: Times Books/Random House, 1989).

20) 'Slow to anger' Referring to God: Ps 86:15; 103:8; 145:8; Neh 9:17;

Joel 2:13; Jonah 4:2

Human anger: Prov. (KJV) 14:29; 15:18; 16:32; Eccl 7:9; Titus 1:7; James 1:19.

21) Ephesians 4:26 (see RSV).

22) A few examples of the use of '*chesed*': Ps 25:6; 63:3; 103:4; Is 63:7; Jer 9:24 (in reference to God).

23) See Ruth 2:20; 3:10 in reference to people.

24) John 1:18; Colossians 1:15.

25) Examples of Jesus expressing feelings: *Anger:* Mark 3:5; John 2:13-17; *Joy:* John 15:11; *Compassion:* Mark 6:34; 8:2; *Tiredness:* John 4:6; *Loneliness:* Matthew 26:56; 27:46; *Discouragement:* John 12:27; *Depression:* Matthew 26:38; Mark 14:34.

26) Examples of Jesus' humour: Matthew 6:34; 7:3–4; 16; 8:22; 15:14; 26; 16:18; 19:24; 23:24; 27. A book that explores this is *The Humour of Christ*, by Elton Trueblood (New York: Harper & Row, 1964).

27) Harry Emerson Fosdick, *The Manhood of the Master* (New York: Association Press, 1958) p 16.

28) Hebrews 4:15 (GNB).

29) Psalm 42:2, 6; 16:9; 22:14; 116:1.

Chapter Seven – Social Wholeness

1) John Donne, 1572–1631. Poet, author, theologion, Dean of St Paul's Cathedral, London. A quote from *Devotions upon Emergent Occasions*, Meditation XVII.

2) M.E. Lamb, 'Father-Infant and Mother-Infant interaction in the first year of life' *Child Development*, 1977, 48: 167–181.

3) See Genesis 1:27 and 2:18.

4) John Powell, *Fully Human, Fully Alive* (Valencia: Tabor, 1976) p 27.

5) See: J.J. Lynch, *The Broken Heart, The Medical Consequences of Loneliness* (New York: Basic Books, 1977).

6) a) C.F. Ortmeyer, *Mortality and Morbidity in the United States* (Cambridge: Harvard University Press, 1974) pp 159–184.
   b) J.J. Lynch, *The Language of the Heart* (New York: Basic Books, 1985) pp 69,70.

7) For further explanation of this, see J. & A. Sturt, *Created for Intimacy* (Guildford: Eagle, 1996) pp 15–17.

8) Richard Foster, *Celebration of Discipline* (London: Hodder & Stoughton, 1983) p 84.

9) Dietrich Bonhoeffer, *Life Together* (London: SCM Press, 1954).

10) Erik Erikson, *Childhood and Society* (St Albans: Triad Paladin, 1977).

11) J. & A. Sturt, *Created for Love* (Guildford: Eagle, 1994).

12) Some excellent books on communication are:

a) John Powell, *Why Am I Afraid To Tell You Who I Am?* (Illinois: Argus, 1977).

b) John Powell & Loretta Brady, *Will The Real Me Please Stand Up?* (Valencia: Tabor, 1985).

c) Robert Bolton, *People Skills* (New Jersey: Prentice-Hall, 1979).

d) See also *Created for Intimacy*, op. cit., Chapter 2.

13) James 1:19.

14) See Job 2:13; 42:8.

15) John Powell & Loretta Brady, *Will the Real Me Please Stand Up* op. cit. p 102.

16) Knowing yourself in these areas is more fully discussed in *Created for Intimacy*, Chapter 5.

17) Introductions to these two tests are found in:

a) M. Goldsmith & M. Wharton, *Knowing Me – Knowing You* (London: SPCK, 1993).

b) D. Riso, *The Enneagram* (London: HarperCollins, 1987).

18) Some books on gender differences are:

a) John Gray, *Men are from Mars, Women are from Venus* (London: HarperCollins, 1992).

b) Deborah Tannen, *You Just Don't Understand* (Australia: Random House, 1990).

c) G. Foster & M. Marshall, *How Can I Get Through To You?* (Australia: Simon & Schuster, 1994).

19) Living-together-loneliness is described further in *Created for Intimacy*, Chapter 1. See also: Dan Kiley, *Living Together, Feeling Alone* (New York: Prentice Hall, 1989).

20) Pedersen, *Cross Cultural Counselling and Psychotherapy* (New York: Pergamon Press, 1981) p 326.

21) Rene Descartes (1596–1650) French mathematician, writer and philosopher who was an influential thinker in the Renaissance.

22) J. Metge & P. Timlock, *Talking Past Each Other* (Wellington: Victoria University Press, revised 1989). A study of the problems of cross-cultural communication in New Zealand.

23) David Augsburger, *Pastoral Counselling Across Cultures* (Philadelphia: Westminster Press, 1986) pp 88ff.

24) James House, *et al.*, 'Social relatonships and health', *Science*, 1988, Vol 241, pp 540–544.

25) Berkman and Syme, 'Social networks, host resistance and mortality', *American Journal of Epidemiology*, 1979, Vol 109) pp 186–204.

26) Susan Kennedy, *et al.*, 'Immunological consequences of acute and chronic stress', *British Journal of Medical Psychology*, 1988, Vol 61, pp 77–85.

27) 1 John 4:20, 21 (The Message).

28) See for example Isaiah 58:6–11; 61:8; Psalm 82:3; 103:6; Jeremiah 7:5–7; 22:3.

29) Exodus 20:1–17.
30) Micah 6:8.
31) Leviticus 19:18.
32) Matthew 22:39; Luke 10:27; Romans 13:9; Galatians 5:14; Ephesians 5:28, 33; James 2:8.
33) Galatians 5:14.
34) Luke 10:25–37.
35) Matthew 5:43, 44.
36) 1 Timothy 5:8.
37) Mark 7:9–13.
38) Some examples are: Ex 22:21; 23:11; Lev 19:10,34; Deut 10: 17–19; 15:7–11; 24:17–21; Ps 35:10; 146:9; Prov 14:31; 17:5; 31:9; Is 58:6–11; James 1:27; 2:1–9.
39) Deuteronomy 10:17,18; Psalm 68:5.
40) Luke 4:18.
41) Matthew 25:31–46.
42) Hebrews 10:24, 25.
43) 1 Corinthians 12:12–31.
44) 1 Corinthians 12:26.
45) Romans 15:7; Ephesians 4:32; Ephesians 4:2; I Thessalonians 5:11; Galatians 6:2.
46) Acts 15:37–40; 2 Timothy 4:11.
47) John 17:9, 11, 21, 23 (our emphasis).
48) Brian Hathaway, *Living Below with the Saints We Know!* (Guildford: Eagle, 1998).
49) J. & A. Sturt, *Created for Intimacy* (Guildford: Eagle, 1994) pp 51–53.
50) J & A. Sturt, *Created for Love* (Guildford: Eagle, 1996) pp 265–270.
51) James Smith & Richard Foster, *A Spiritual Formation Handbook* (San Francisco: Harper, 1993). A Renovaré resource for spiritual growth.
52) Acts 2:42–47; 5:42; 10:22; 12:12; 16:15, 32; 18:26; 28:30; Romans 16:5; Colossians 4:15; Philemon 2.
53) Two helpful books on home groups and how to run them are:
a) John Mallison, *Growing Christians in Small Groups* (Sydney: ANZEA, 1989).
b) Neal McBride, *How to Lead Small Groups* (Colorado: Navpress, 1990).
54) Hebrews 10:25.
55) D. Clark, *Basic Communities, Towards an Alternative Society* (London: SPCK, 1977) pp 4–5.
56) K. McCamant and C. Durrett, *Cohousing: A Contemporary Approach to Housing Ourselves* (Berkley: Habitat Press, 1988).
57) Jean Vanier, *Community and Growth* (London: DLT, 1989) p 22.
58) Kingdom values and the qualities of true community are defined in Philippians 2:1–5.

Chapter Eight – Spiritual Wholeness

1) Blaise Pascal (1623–1662) French mathematician, physicist, writer and religious philosopher.

2) An ancient story quoted by David Runcorn in *Space for God* (London: Daybreak, 1990) p 55.

3) St Augustine of Hippo, *Confessions,* Book 1, Chapter 1

4) Aleksander Solzhenitsyn, 1918 – Russian novelist, historian and Nobel prize winner in Literature.

5) 1 Corinthians 13:12 (The Message).

6) Romans 1:20; Hebrews 1:1–3; John 1:14

7) John 14:6–11.

8) In Scripture God is frequently represented by feminine metaphors. For example, Deuteronomy 32:18; Isaiah 49:15; 42:14; 66:13; Matthew 23:37.

9) Matthew 22:37-40.

10) Gerard Hughes, *God of Surprises* (London: Dartman, Longman & Todd, 1985) p 39.

11) Luke 2:52.

12) John 14:16–26; 16:7–14; Romans 8:26,27; Philippians 3:10.

13) e.g: Acts 4:8, 31; 6:5; 9:31; 19:6

14) John 1:1, 14.

15) 1 Corinthians 2:10–14.

16) Jeremiah 12:2.

17) John 5:39, 40.

18) See J & A Sturt, *Created for Love* (Guildford: Eagle, 1994) Chapter 4.

19) Gordon Dahl, *Work, Play and Worship in a Leisure-Oriented Society* (Minneapolis: Augsburg Publishing, 1972) p 12.

20) Wayne Oates, *Confessions of a Workaholic* (Nashville: Abingdon, 1971) p 5.

21) 1 Timothy 6:17; Psalm 34:9,10; 84:11; Acts 14:17.

22) Matthew 19:23–29. See also Matthew 6:19-24; Proverbs 30:8; Jeremiah 9:23,24.

23) The 'prosperity gospel' is evaluated in *The Health and Wealth Gospel* by Bruce Barron (Downers Grove: InterVarsity Press, 1987).

24) Matthew 6:21 & 24 See also 1 Timothy 6:5.

25) Sanaya Roman, *Spiritual Growth – Being Your Higher Self* (Tiburn: Kramer, 1989) p 9.

26) J.B. Phillips, *Your God Is Too Small* (London: Epworth, 1952).

27) Acts 11:26; 26:28; 1 Peter 4:16.

28) Dietrich Bonhoeffer, *The Cost of Discipleship* (London: SCM Press, 1954).

29) Suzanne Zuercher, *Enneagram Spirituality* (Notre Dame, Indiana: Ave Maria Press, 1992) p 135.

30) John 5:19, 30; 8:28.
31) John 16:23 (The Message).
32) Dom Chapman, quoted by Richard Foster in *Prayer* (London: Hodder & Stoughton, 1992) p 7.
33) Ruth Burrows, *Before the Living God – Prayer and Practice* (London: Sheed & Ward, 1988) p 101.
34) Ephesians 3:20.
35) Evelyn Underhill, *The Essentials of Mysticism* (Oxford: Oneworld Publications, 1995).
36) Romans 12:1.
37) 1 Corinthians 14:15.
38) Psalms 34:3; 95:6.
39) John 4:24.
40) Matthew 6:9–13.
41) Thomas Green, *Opening to God* (Notre Dame, Indianna: Ave Maria, 1992) p 17.
42) 1 Kings 19:12,13; Jeremiah 7:13; Matthew 2:13; Acts 9:3,4.
43) Matthew 6:6.
44) See Richard Foster, op. cit., 128, 129.
45) Joyce Huggett, *Open to God* (Guildford: Eagle, 1997).
46) Isaiah 43:1.
47) Ephesians 6:18.
48) Michael & Norrisey, *Prayer and Temperament* (Charlottesville: The Open Door, 1991) p 20.
49) Mark Virkler, *Dialogue with God* (South Plainfield: Bridge, 1986).
50) Ruth Burrows, *Ascent to Love* (London: DLT, 1991) p 60.
51) Matthew 6:6.
52) David Runcorn, op. cit., p. 7.
53) Henri Nouwen, *Out of Solitude* (Notre Dame, Indiana: Ave Maria Press, 1990) p 21, 22.
54) Psalm 1:2; 119:97.
55) See Psalms 119:15, 23; 143:5; 145:5
56) Job 26:14.
57) Richard of St Victor.
58) Psalm 46:10; 62:1.
59) Richard Foster, op cit p 166.
60) Quoted by Karen Karpa, *Where God Begins to Be* (Grand Rapids: Eerdmans, 1994).
61) John of the Cross, Canticle st. 1, quoted by Ruth Burrows, *Ascent to Love*, op. cit. p 24.
62) Psalm 23:2
63) See Mark Virkler, op. cit.
64) Margaret Magdelen, in *Keeping a Spiritual Journal*, ed Edward England (Godalming: Highland, 1991) p 82.
65) See J & A Sturt, *Created for Intimacy* (Guildford: Eagle, 1996) pp 101–105.

66) Some helpful books on understanding dreams:

  a) Morton Kelsey, *Dreams: A Way to Listen to God* (New York: Paulist Press, 1982).

  b) Herman Riffel, *Your Dreams: God's Neglected Gift* (Lincoln: Chosen Books, 1981).

  c) Russ Parker, *Healing Dreams* (London: SPCK, 1988).

  d) Savary, Berne & Williams, *Dreams and Spiritual Growth* (New Jersey: Paulist Press, 1984).

  e) Margaret Bowater, *Dreams and Visions, Language of the Spirit* (Auckland: Tendem, 1997).

67) Savary, Berne & Willams, op. cit., p. 71.

68) See Margaret Guenther, *Holy Listening: The Art of Spiritual Direction* (London: DLT, 1992) Chapter 3.

69) Galatians 4:19.

70) Ruth Burrows, *Before the Living God* (London: Sheed & Ward, 1988) p 118.

Chapter Nine – Towards Wholeness & Maturity

1) Irenaeus, c. 120-200 AD, leading theologian of the second century, Bishop of Lugdunum, chief opponent of the Gnostic heresy. He advanced the development of the canon of Scripture that we know today.

2) C.S. Lewis, *The Silver Chair* (Middlesex: Puffin, 1953) Chapter 2.

3) John Hawkesby, *Save the Last Dance for Me* (London: Hodder & Stoughton, 1997) p 97.

4) Yeast is used by Jesus to refer to the positive way the Kingdom of God grows (Luke 13:21) and by Paul to illustrate negative influences (1 Corinthians 5:6; Galatians 5:9).

5) Ephesians 4:13, 12, 16.

6) Ecclesiastes 3:1–8.

7) Philippians 3:13,14.

8) Richard Foster, *Celebration of Discipline* (London: Hodder & Stoughton, 1983) p 164.

9) John 15:11.

10) Philippians 3:12 (TLB).

SELECTED BIBLIOGRAPHY

The following are helpful books which expand on some of the subjects discussed in this book.

Created for Love by John and Agnes Sturt (Guildford: Eagle, 1994).

This addresses the issue of self-esteem, from a psychological and biblical perspective. Practical ways of growing in self-worth are described. It is a workbook, designed for use by individuals on their own, with a counsellor or in small groups.

Created for Intimacy by John and Agnes Sturt (Guildford: Eagle, 1996).

This book looks at the experience of loneliness, friendship and intimacy in a survey of 300 people. The basic principles, keys and blocks to intimacy are defined. Intimacy in singleness, marriage and in our relationship with God are explored in practical ways. It is a workbook for individual or group use.

Created to Be Whole builds on concepts outlined in our two previous books in this series.

Wellness Workbook by Regina Ryan and John Travis (Berkley: Ten Speed Press, 1981).

A feast of information on how to take responsibility for our health and wellness. It expands on the first four chapters of *Created to be Whole*. Some of the concepts may not totally fit a Christian perspective, but when you eat fish you don't have to swallow the bones.

Growing Christians in Small Groups by John Mallison (London: ANZEA/Joint Board of Christian Education, 1989).

The Church started as a small group movement. This book describes the value of small groups in church growth, and how to run them, and is full of practical advice and insights gained from 35 years of ministry.

Community and Growth by Jean Vanier (London: DLT, 1979).
The author is founder of the L'Arche communities, caring for and living in community with mentally handicapped people. This book is an introduction to community living, and is full of spiritual insights and practical wisdom.

The Seven Habits of Highly Successful People by Steven Covey (Melbourne: The Business Library, 1990).
A book filled with practical wisdom for those seeking a balanced, healthy lifestyle. Covey bases his principles of success in life and in business on lasting values and a 'character ethic', which is essentially drawn from biblical teaching.

First Things First by Steven Covey and Roger Merrill (New York: Simon & Schuster, 1994).
Covey builds on his previous book, showing how to maintain a healthy balance in setting goals and in focusing on what is important in life, not just the urgent. Wholeness flows from 'principle-centred' living, in family life as well as in business.

The Stress of Life by Hans Selye (New York: McGraw-Hill, 1976).
This famous classic is written by a physician who spent his lifetime studying the effects of stress on the human body, and how to understand and manage stress. It is written in a scientific but clear way for both the professional and lay reader.

When I Relax I Feel Guilty by Tim Hansel (Elgin, Illinois: David Cook, 1979).
A humorous and profound look at some principles of healthy, relaxed and godly living. It dispels the myths: 'Fatigue is next to godliness' and 'The harder you work, the more God loves you'. He shows the difference between leisure and idleness.

Your Magnificent Mind by Gary Collins (Grand Rapids:

Baker, 1988).

A Christian psychologist provides many fascinating and accurate insights into the human brain and how our minds work. Exhaustive references make this a valuable resource for those wishing to read further on the subject.

Man's Search for Meaning by Viktor Frankl (New York: Simon & Schuster, revised 1984).

A challenging story of a psychiatrist's experiences in Auschwitz and other Nazi concentration camps. His philosophy grew from this: finding meaning is the primary human motivational force, and that a reason to live promotes health and wholeness.

Celebration of Discipline by Richard Foster (London: Hodder & Stoughton, 1983).

Indispensable reading for anyone interested in spiritual growth. Foster describes thirteen spiritual disciplines, including some we discuss in Chapter Eight of *Created to be Whole*. A stimulating guide for personal devotional life and a resource book for group study.

Celebrating the Disciplines by Richard Foster and Kathryn Yanni (London: Harper & Row, 1992).

A practical workbook to help the reader develop the disciplines outlined in *Celebration of Discipline*. It provides challenging exercises and fresh material to cover a year's devotional programme.

Will the Real Me Please Stand Up by John Powell & Loretta Brady (Valencia, Tabor Publishing, 1985).

The authors describe twenty-five guidelines for good communication and outline the principles of how to share myself and accept the sharing of others. A practical and easy-to-read book on the essential skills of good communication.

Fully Human, Fully Alive by John Powell (Valencia: Tabor, 1976).

Our expectations, feelings and reactions are determined by our 'vision' or belief system: how we view ourselves, others, life, the world and God. For wholeness, we need to change any distortions of our vision, and Powell shows us how to do this.

The Christian Vision – The Truth that Sets Us Free by John Powell (Allen: Argus, 1984).

A challenging book for understanding yourself, others, the world, God, suffering, the Church and the will of God. Full of insights that will stretch you in assessing your values and making changes.

Living Below with the Saints We Know by Brian Hathaway (Guildford, Eagle, 1997).

This book looks at the important, but neglected issue of relationships in the Church. Brian writes from many years experience of pastoring and provides practical and biblical insights into relationships in congregational life.

People Skills by Robert Bolton (New Jersey: Prentice-Hall, 1979).

This standard text is a comprehensive coverage of inter-personal communication skills, exploring the essentials of listening, reflecting, assertiveness and conflict management.

Pastoral Counseling Across Cultures by David Augsburger (Philadelphia: Westminster Press, 1986).

A wealth of information and wisdom, providing an understanding of different cultures from sound biblical and psycho-social perspectives. Essential reading for all Christian workers in today's multicultural world.

The Freedom of Forgiveness by David Augsburger (Chicago: Moody, revised 1988).

A life-changing book about the importance and power of forgiveness, essential to spiritual health and growth to wholeness. The author shows why and how we must forgive others and make forgiveness a way of life.

Prayer, the Transforming Friendship by James Houston (Oxford: Lion, 1989).

Houston says: 'Prayer in the full light of knowing about

ourselves is vitally important to sustain our life in all its different dimensions.' This book helps in that understanding and experience of prayer, from the difficulties to the reality of prayer.

To Believe in Jesus by Ruth Burrows (London: Sheed and Ward, 1991).

This book brings us through learning to know Jesus in his humanity to experiencing his life in us, and growing into holiness. This is God's work, as we abandon ourselves to him.

Formed by the Desert by Joyce Huggett (Guildford: Eagle, 1997).

All who have encountered God in 'desert experiences' come out paradoxically richer and with a deep and transformed faith. This book is beautifully illustrated with desert photography.

SCRIPTURE REFERENCES

GENESIS   1:25,27, 31; 2:7; 2:18; 4:5-8; 6:5; 8:21.
EXODUS   20:1-17; 20:8-11; 21:24; 22:21; 23:11; 32:19.
LEVITICUS   19:10,18,34.
NUMBERS   22:27.
DEUTERONOMY10:17-19; 15:7-11; 24:17-21.
RUTH   2:20; 3:10.
1 KINGS   Ch 18, 19.
1 CHRONICLES 29:18.
NEHEMIAH   9:17.
JOB   2:13; 26:14; 42:8.
PSALMS   1:2; 16:9; 18:20; 22:14; 23:2; 25:5; 25:6; 34:3; 35:10;
                 42:2,6; 43:9,10; 46:10; 55:22; 62:1; 63:3; 68:5; 82:3;
                 84:11; 86:15; 95:6; 103:4; 103:6; 103:8; 112:5; 116:1;
                 119:15, 23, 97; 127:1; 139:14; 143:5; 145:5, 8; 146:9;
                 147:11.
PROVERBS   11:24,25; 14:29; 14:31; 15:13,15; 15:18; 16:32; 17:5;
                 17:22; 29:18; 30:8; 31:9.
ECCLESIASTES 3:1-8; 7:9; 9:10; 11:1
ISAIAH   26:3; 43:1; 54:2; 58:6-11; 61:8; 63:7.
JEREMIAH   7:5-7; 7:13; 9:23,24; 12:2; 22:3.
JOEL   2:13; 2:28.
JONAH   4:1-4.
MICAH   6:8.
MATTHEW   2:13; 5:4; 5:9; 5:23,24; 5:38; 5:43,44; 5:48; 6:6, 9-13;
                 6:12,14; 6:19-24; 6:25-34; 7:3,4; 7:13,14; 7:16; 8:22;
                 11:29; 13:3,10,13, 34,35,53; 15:14,26; 16:18; 16:25;
                 18:21,22; 18:21-35; 19:23-29; 22:37-40; 23:11;
                 23:24,27; 25:31-46; 26:38; 26:56; 27:46.
MARK   1:41; 2:27; 3:5; 4:35-41; 5:34; 5:41; 6:34; 6:56; 7:9-13;
                 7:33; 8:2; 8:22-25; 8:35; 9:42; 10:13-16; 10:35-45;
                 14:34.
LUKE   2:52; 4:18; 4:31-37; 4:40; 6:27-42; 6:38; 7:1-10; 7:14;
                 8:19-21; 8:48; 9:23-25; 9:24; 9:46-48; 10:25-37;
                 10:27; 12:32-34; 13:13; 13:21; 14:26,27; 15:1-32;
                 17:33; 12:35; 17:19; 19:1-9; 19:8-9; 22:24-27; 22:51.
JOHN   1:1,14; 1:18; 2:13-17; 4:6; 4:24; 5:1-15; 5:19,30; 5:35;
                 5:39,40; 8:1-11; 8:28,29; 8:32; 8:46; 10:10; 12:25;
                 12:27; 13:1; 13:3-7;13:23-25; 13:34,35; 14:6-11;
                 14:15-17; 14:16-26; 14:27; 15:11; 16:7-14; 16:13;

	16:23; 17:9,11,21,23; 20:19,26.
ACTS	2:17; 2:42-27; 4:8,31; 5:42; 6:5,6; 8:17; 9:3,4; 9:17; 9:31; 10:22; 11:26; 12:12; 13:3; 14:7; 15:37-40; 16:15,32; 18:26; 19:6; 26:28; 28:8; 28:30.
ROMANS	1:20; 2:5-8; 5:3,4; 6:12,13; 7:18; 8:6; 8:8; 8:26,27; 8:29; 12:1,2; 12:15; 13:9; 15:1-3; 15:7; 16:5.
1 CORINTHIANS	2:10-14; 2:14-16; 3:10-15; 5:6; 6:13,19,20; 9:27; 12:12-31; 13:2; 13:12; 14:15; 14:20; 15:44.
2 CORINTHIANS	5:9; 5:21; 6:16; 10:4,5; 10:12.
GALATIANS	1:10; 4:4; 4:19; 5:9; 5:14; 5:17; 5:22; 6:2; 6:4; 6:5.
EPHESIANS	1:18; 3:20; 4:2; 4:13; 4:12,16; 4:15; 4:22; 4:23,24; 4:26; 4:32; 5:28,33; 6:18.
PHILIPPIANS	1:6; 1:7; 2:4; 2:5-11; 3:10; 3:12; 3:13,14; 4:7; 4:8; 4:11,12.
COLOSSIANS	1:15; 1:28,29; 3:23; 4:15.
1 THESSALONIANS	5:6-8; 5:11.
1 TIMOTHY	3:16; 5:8; 6:5, 6; 6:17.
2 TIMOTHY	1:6; 1:7; 2:15; 3:16; 4:11.
TITUS	1:7; 2:1-12.
PHILEMON	2
HEBREWS	1:1-3; 4:15; 6:1; 6:2; 6:19; 10:24,25; 11:1; 12:11; 12:15.
JAMES	1:2-4; 1:3-5; 1:12; 1:19; 1:27; 2:1-9; 3:17,18; 4:8; 5:14; 5:15.
1 PETER	1:6,7; 1:13; 2:2; 4:7; 4:16; 5:7; 5:8; 5:14.
2 PETER	1:6.
1 JOHN	4:2; 4:20,21.

SUBJECT INDEX

A-B-C model of behaviour, 29
Abuse, 68,171
Acceptance, 169
Actors–Reactors , 25, 121
Addictions, 164
Adrenal exhaustion, 53
Alexithymia, 148
Alzheimer's disease, 18
Anger, 61, 154-157, 160
Anorexia nervosa, 94
Anxiety, 105, 130-131, 146
Archimedes, 115
Aristotle, 153
Attitudes, 41, 80, 115-121, 130, 131, 190
Augsburger, David, 78
Augustine, Saint, 81, 184, 196
Autonomy, 164
Awareness –
    self-awareness, 24, 75, 90-91, 164,
    spiritual awareness, 80-81

Baggage, internal, 55-56, 61, 68
Balance, 16-17, 25-26, 104, 179, 212-215
Becoming, 9, 14
Beliefs, 28-29
Belonging, 162, 183
Bible, 89-90, 175, 187
Bitterness, 55, 70-71, 78
Blocks to wholeness, Chapter 3
Body –
    biblical perspectives, 89,
    'body-life', 177-182
    image, 87
    listening to, 52, 60, 91
    physiology, 88-89

Bonhoeffer, Dietrich, 164, 191
Boundaries, 166
Brain –
    description, 17, 112-115
    deterioration, 18
    left and right brain, 109, 113-115, 120
Brand, Paul, 52
Burnt-out –
    causes, 119
    Inventory Test, 58, 62
    recovery, 54-55
    Prevention Assessment, 59-61
    reversing burnout, 59-61
    stages, 56-5 7
    symptoms, 55, 57
    treatment, 57,59
Busyness, 43, 96, 164, 188-189

Calories, 97, 100
Cancer, 51, 94, 96, 98, 145
Carbohydrates, 94
Celebration of life, 215
Change, 14-15, 40-41, 47, 59, 62, 69, 72-73, 122, 132-133
Choice, 28
Cholesterol, 47
Christian –
    behaviour, 44, 155
    Care Centre, 76
    communities, 181-182
    faith/model, 20, 157, 191
    life, 34, 43, 124, 131, 209
Church –
    relationships, 177-179
    home groups, 180
Clinebell, Howard, 30
Co-dependence, 166
Collins, Gary, 113

Commitment, 122
Community, 32, 177-182, 211
Communication, 60, 167-170
Comparisons, 16
Compartmentalising, 190
Compassion fatigue, 45
Conflict, 170-172, 178
Conformity, 42
Contemplation, 199
Contentment, 121
Control –
    of feelings, 140, 143-145
    of self, 61, 122, 131, 136
Control-Demand model of
stress, 130-132
Controlling, 246, 253, 257, 294,
698
Coué, Emil, 118
Counselling, 170
Counselling, 9, 30, 76, 167, 203
Covey, Steven, 40, 125
Cultural differences, 103, 115,
173-174

'Dead-lines', 40
Dependence, 166
Depression, 53
Desert Fathers/Mothers, 195
Diets, 61, 94-99
Dietary supplements, 98
Disciple, 191
Disciplined thinking, 120-121
Discontent, healthy, 74
Diseases, stress related, 50-51
Disease-prone personality, 146
Distress, 49-50
DNA, 25, 88
Donne, John, 162
Dreams, 105-106, 202-203, 206
'Drivers' personal, 39, 42-46, 54,
107
Drugs, 28, 50
Dualism, 87

Effective living model, 123
Einstein, Albert, 115, 117

Elijah and burn-out, 53
Eliot, T.S., 39
Ellis, Albert, 28
Emotions –
    developement, 18
    emotional maturity, 148-157
    emotional immaturity, 70
    somatisation of emotions, 76
    understanding emotions,
    137
Empowering, 30
Encouragement, 180-181
Endorphins, 93, 102, 120
Enneagram, 170
Enthusiasm, 119
Environment, 32
Erikson, Erik, 164
Eu-stress, 48, 50
Exercise –
    aerobic 60, 100-102
    Benefits of, 101-103

Fats, 94
Fear, 72, 138, 144-145
Feelings –
    accepting feelings, 140-141
    basic feelings, 138
    cognitive labelling of
    emotions, 139-140
    contract, 152
    controlling feelings, 143
    describing feelings, 159
    feelings and emotions,
    138
    feelings and emotional
    health, 146-147
    feelings and faith, 157-158,
    161
    feelings and Jesus, 157
    feelings and physical
    health, 144-145
    feelings and relationships,
    147-148
    language of feelings, 148
    owning feelings, 142
    processing feelings, 150

thoughts and feelings, 138
Fellowship, 179, 191
Fibre, 96
Food pyramid, 97, 99
Forgiveness, 61, 78, 83
Foster, Richard, 179, 199
Frankl, Viktor, 27, 118
Free radical damage, 98
Friendship, 60

Gandhi, Mahatma, 19-20
Gender differences, 170
Generous thinking, 116
Genetics, 16-17
Glasser, William, 28
Goal-setting, 60, 122-129
    frustrated goals, 127-129
    goal-setting process, 124-26
    types of goals, 123
God –
    belief in, 118
    fatherhood/motherhood,
    81, 186
    his control, 118, 120, 130
    his feelings, 153, 155, 157
    his forgiveness, 79
    his image, 89, 142, 162
    his work in the world
    and us, 36, 69, 72, 78, 118,
    124, 131, 185, 189, 197,
    198, 198, 199
    listening to God, 164, 194,
    203
    personal relationship
    with, 19, 30, 31, 35, 123-
    124, 203-205
    small view of God, 190-191
Goleman, Daniel, 146
Greek philosophy, 87, 89, 91,
140
Grief, 55, 71-72
Groups, 179-181
Growth, emotional, 18, 148-157
    intellectual, 17-18, 26
    physical, 17
    social, 18-19, 169

spiritual, 19
Growth counselling, 30
Guilt, 43

Hal, 16
Happiness, 121
Hathaway, Brian, 178
Health education, 24
Hebrew thinking, 31-32, 88
Heraclitus, 41
Hillel, 32
Hippocrates, 91
Hobbies, 61, 107
Holy Spirit, 35, 91, 104, 162,
186-187, 200, 204
Honesty, 150
Huggett, Joyce, 195
Human development potential,
16-20
Humour, 119
Hurry sickness, 46
Hurts of the past, 61, 68, 71, 76

'Illth', Chapter 2
Imagination, 120, 221-222
Immune response, 51, 98, 174
Independence, 166
Individualism, 173
Insomnia, 105
Intellectual development, 17
Inter-dependence, 166
Intimacy, 60, 157
Irenaeus, St, 208

James, William, 80
Jesus, 32-33, 104, 116, 157, 185-
186, 195
Jogging, 100
John the Baptist, 59
Journalling, 200

Laing, R.D., 41
Laughter, 61
Lectio Divina, 195
Leprosy, 52
Lewis, C.S., 208

Life expectancy, 25, 153, 174
Lifestyle, 39, 54
Listening, 167
Logotherapy, 28
Loneliness, 103, 163
Loss, 71
Love, 150

Mace, David and Vera, 53
Marcus Aurelius, 112
Marginalised people, 178
Marriage, 124, 147, 170-171
Maslow, Abraham, 26, 87
Materialism, 46, 189
Maternal Deprivation
Syndrome, 103
Maturity, 34, 169
Meaning in life, 27, 30
Medical world view alterna-
tives, 30
    Western medical model,
    20-22
    Animistic illness model,
    20-21
    Wellness model, 23-25
Meditation, 114, 198-200
Melatonin, 105
Mental attitudes, 115-121
Merton, Thomas, 199
Messiah complex, 45
Mid-life crisis, 74
Mind-Body Medicine, 22, 76,
146
Modelling, 67, 147-148
Mourning, 71
Myers-Briggs Test, 170

Needs, basic, 87
Neitzsche, Fredrich, 30
New age thinking, 189-190
Nouwen, Henri, 198
Nutrition, 91-99
    Dietary supplements, 97
    contamination of food,
    91-92
    contamination of water, 92

How we eat, 98-99
What we eat, 94-98, 110
Why we eat, 92-93

Open-mindedness, 117
Optimism, 118-119
Other-centredness, 19, 26, 165-
166, 169, 209
Otium sanctum, 104
Outward thinking, 117-118
Overweight, 93-95
Pain, 52
Papua New Guinea, 20, 146,
187
Parental model, 43
Pascal, Blaise, 184
Pauling, Linus, 98
Peace, 31-32, 121
Peale, Norman Vincent, 118
Peck, Scott, 16
People-pleasing, 44
Perfection, 34
Performance pressure, 42
Personality types, 46-47, 197
Phillips, J.B., 190
Physical –
    deterioration, 17
    fitness, 17
    growth, 17
Plato, 22, 87
Poor-me syndrome, 71
Poor people, 183
Positive thinking, 118
Powell, John, 137, 147, 169
Prayer –
    nature of, 131-132, 194-196
    Augustinian prayer, 196
    centering prayer, 196
    Ignation prayer, 196
    Lectio Divina, 195
    for healing, 77
    ways of prayer, 194-199
Proteins, 96
Psychological models of well-
ness, 26
Psychoneuroimmunology, 145

Psychosomatic, 22
Quantum physics, 88

Rational Emotive Therapy, 28
Reality Therapy, 28
Relationships, 175-179
Relaxation, 60, 104-109
    breathing, 108, 219-222
    exercises, 221-224
    of muscles, 108-109, 220-221
'Re-member', 77
Renaissance, 173
Renewing the mind, 35, 131-134, 136
Renovaré groups, 179
Rescuing, 44-46
Respect, 168-169, 175
Responsibility, 25, 73, 141-143
Responsibility for wholeness, 35-36
Rest and Recreation, 104-109, 111
Rest day, 106
Retreats, 199-200
Risk-taking, 24, 75-76

Salvation, 32-34
Self-actualisation, 26-27
Self-awareness (See awareness)
Self-centredness, 165-166
Self-esteem, 61, 69-70, 165
Selye, Hans, 48
Seneca, 13
Sexual identity, 90
Shalom, 31-32
Sheol, 32
Silence, 107, 201
Sleep, 60, 105, 222
Social –
    Christian faith perspec-
    tives, 175-179
    cultural perspectives, 173-174
    development, 18, 164-166
    isolation, 163-164
    Readjustment scale, 41

    relationship, 166-169
Socrates, 157
Solitude, 107, 164, 195-200
Solzhenitsyn, Alexander 184
Sophocles, 87
Spirit, 54, 116-117, 120, 122, 124, 158, 166, 189, 255, 257, 265-266, 268-270, 272,
Spiritual development,19, 80
Spiritual Direction, 203, 206, 207
Stoics, 140
Stress –
    assessing, 49
    diseases, 50-51
    eu-stress, 50-51
    relief, 101, 103-104
    symptoms, 49-50, 55
    understanding, 48, 128-129

'telios', 3-34, 212
Tielhard de Chardin, 9
Time, 40
Time out, 58, 106
Tony and Jan's story, 13, 14, 44, 102-103, 128, 156, 171-172, 190, 209
Touch –
    benefits, 103
    deprivation, 103
    healthy and unhealthy, 61, 104
    laying on of hands, 104
    modelling by Jesus, 104
Tournier, Paul, 74
Transcendence, 173
Travis, Dr John, 23
Trust, basic, 164
Truth, 131
Type-A/Type-B personality, 46-47, 52

Unforgiveness, 70-71

Vacations, 60, 106
Values, 29, 31, 55

Vanier, Jean,182
Vision –
    expanding, 73-82,117
    lack of, 66-68
    statement, 82
Vitamins, 96,98

Weight control, 61,94-96, 100-101
Wellness, 23-26
Wholeness –
    blocks, 66-73
    Christian model, 32-35
    community, 211
    definition, 9-10, 14-16, 34, 217
    emotional, Chapter 6
    intellectual, Chapter 5
    Jewish model, 31-32
    keys to wholeness, 73-81
    medical model, 20-23
    personal, 210
    physical, Chapter 4
    psychological model, 26-31
    relational, 210-211
    social, Chapter 7
    spiritual, Chapter 8
    wellness model, 23-26
'Wholth', Chapter 1
Witch-doctor, 21
Workaholism, 43-44, 54, 64, 188
World Health Organisation, 20
World view, 16, 29
Worrying, 237, 308
Worship, 35, 193-194, 197

Yancey, Philip, 52
Yerke's curve, 49-51

CREATED FOR LOVE

JOHN AND AGNES STURT

You want the truth? Most of us don't like ourselves very much. And we suspect that God doesn't either . . . Do yourself a favour. Read this book and let the Sturts' insights work magic on your soul.
John Cooney, Grapevine

How does a person develop better self-esteem?
How do they enter into more secure
relationships?
How can a lifetime's behavioural patterns
be changed?

People with low self-esteem carry around a constant pain inside which produces self-preoccupation. True self-worth starts with the awareness of being created in the image of God and of being of great value and worth to him.

Created for Love is a practical manual with questions for personal reflection and specific exercises at the end of each chapter, written simply and effectively and drawn upon many years' counselling experience.

0 86347 164 1

CREATED FOR INTIMACY

JOHN AND AGNES STURT

- Why do I find it so hard to experience oneness with others?
- How do I enjoy intimacy with another?

In our materialistic society there is a temptation to love things and use people. Friendship and intimacy only become priorities when we love people and use things. If you are interested in how to be close to another person, whether single or married, this book may help you. Experiencing human intimacy prepares us for intimacy with God and intimacy with him transforms human relationships.

Created for Intimacy is a practical book with questions and exercises at the end of each chapter. It can be used on your own, with another person or in a group.

John and Agnes Sturt help us by suggesting ways of finding tailor-made answers that could contain healing and wholeness. Throughout the book they point the way to the architect of intimacy: God.
JOYCE AND DAVID HUGGETT, **from the Preface**

0 86347 188 9